Saltwater Fly Fishing
for
Pacific Salmon

To my fly fishing partners who were there:
Barry, Bob, Fran, Jack, Jim & Jim, Lew, Martin,
Marilyn, Ralph, Richard, Roy, Terry.

Saltwater Fly Fishing
for
Pacific Salmon

Barry M. Thornton

Fisher '89

hancock

house

ISBN 0-88839-319-9
Copyright © 1995 Barry M. Thornton

ISBN 0-88839-376-8 Limited Edition

Cataloging in Publication Data
Thornton, Barry M.
  Saltwater fly fishing for Pacific Salmon

  ISBN 0-88839-319-9

  1. Pacific salmon fishing—British Columbia.   2. Saltwater fly fishing—British Columbia.   I. Title.
SH686.T56 1994   799.1'755   C94-910742-5

Edited: Suzanne M. Chin
Production: Myron Shutty and Jeffrey Stilz
Photographs: Author
Illustrations: W. J. (Jim) Fisher

Also by Barry Thornton: *Steelhead, the Supreme Trophy Trout*

Published simultaneously in Canada and the United States by

HANCOCK HOUSE PUBLISHERS LTD.
19313 Zero Avenue, Surrey, B.C. V4P 1M7
(604) 538-1114   Fax (604) 538-2262

HANCOCK HOUSE PUBLISHERS
1431 Harrison Avenue, Blaine, WA 98230-5005
(604) 538-1114   Fax (604) 538-2262

Contents

Introduction 7

1 Hunting for Salmon
  Introduction 11
  A Key to Salmon Hunting Conditions 25

2 The Fish!
  Family Salmonidae, Genus *Oncorhynchus*
  Introduction 27
  Coho Salmon *(O. kisutch)* 32
  Pink Salmon *(O. gorbuscha)* 36
  Chinook Salmon *(O. tschawytscha)* 46

3 Fly Casting on Open Salt Water
  Introduction 53
  Chase Casting 57
  Open Water Anchoring 60
  Hunt-Drift-Cast for Early Coho 65

4 Beach and Estuary Fly Fishing
  Autumn Beach Fly Fishing for Coho 89
  Midsummer Estuary Fly Casting for Pinks . . . 97

5 Tackle and Equipment 105

6 Saltwater Flies
  Introduction 115
  A Selection of Successful Salmon Patterns . . 127

7 An Alphabetical Creel of Tips 135

8 Salmon and Angler Management 151

9 Eternal Memories
  Quadra Island Coho Fly Fishing 161

Introduction

The Pacific coast provides many opportunities for the saltwater salmon fly fisherman. Pacific Northwest anglers are currently targeting the various salmon species with considerable success. This book focuses on fly fishing methods for catching these species along with the many experiences I've had in my pursuit of this challenging and exciting form of fly fishing.

Until recently, little has been written about saltwater fly fishing for Pacific salmon. It is, unquestionably, a sophisticated fly-angling choice for the fly fisherman that comes after many successful conventional salmon fishing experiences. It is not new, but an angling practice many pioneers attempted, some very successfully, however it has not been followed up as it should! It is probably a symptom of our times—our pioneering spirit—that, now that we have resolved the skills and techniques needed for consistently successful river and lake fishing, we are now searching for new waters in which to test our mettle. Fortunately, lying at our doorstep is the open water of the vast Pacific Ocean. Improvements in boats and motors and the evolution in fly fishing lines, rods, and fly-tying materials have given the fly fisherman the tools and the access to the fish.

How fortunate we are to have such a family of fish, the genus Oncorhynchus, the Pacific salmons inhabiting these waters. These various species of Pacific salmon inhabit the infinite fjords, inlets, islands and estuaries of the north Pacific coast waiting, just waiting for the inevitable rush of fly fishermen who have mastered challenging and pleasurable trout experiences in freshwater lakes and streams and now, satiated, search for new waters and experiences.

How well I remember one summer day when I took a seasoned trout fly fisherman saltwater fly fishing for salmon! In no time he was hooking and beaching bright two- and three-kilogram coho salmon as if he had done it regularly for years. While he had the skills, he lacked the opportunity or the time to use these skills in a saltwater location where there were feeding salmon. The thrill we shared was immense and when a very large spring salmon ran and ran and ran, finally breaking his leader just before he had run out all the reel's backing, I witnessed that fly fisherman's incredulity at what he was experiencing. It was that simple.

There is no trick to saltwater fly fishing for salmon; all the skills of casting, retrieving the fly, and locating the fish remain essentially the same. In fact the simplicity of the fly patterns used—the simpler the better—astound seasoned fly fisherman.

I firmly believe that any angler who has learned the skills of fly fishing can and will be effective at saltwater fly fishing for salmon if he spends the same time on the water fly fishing as he would using the conventional salmon fishing methods of drift fishing, mooching or trolling. In those major areas of calmer salt water where salmon fishermen concentrate, areas around kelp beds or shallow water, I would venture that the angler will be even more successful fly fishing. If there is any secret, it likely lies in the angling truism of placing the fly in the areas where there are fish and keeping the fly in the water more times than it is out!

In this book I have concentrated on only three of the six salmon species; the coho (silver), the chinook (king, spring, tyee) and the pink (humpback). Of the other three species, the masu only inhabits the waters of Asia on and near Japan and seems to exhibit similar traits to the coho. The other two, the sockeye and the chum, are more commercial species available to the fly fisherman only at specific times of the year. A sockeye fly fishery is presently evolving in salt waters where these fish congregate before moving into fresh water. One highly publicized water is the Alberni Inlet on Vancouver Island, British Columbia during July. Pink and deep red patterns appear to be the most successful for these fish. The chum salmon does not frequent accessible waters except during its final run to its natal stream and rarely presents itself in saltwater fly fishing areas but, every year, I hear of a new salmon fly fishery at some estuary along the British Columbia coast.

This is a book about experiences with salmon; about flies and success; about equipment and experimentation; about water and weather; in short, it is a book with considerable "how-to!" It is also, like my earlier book on steelhead, a labor of love.

1

Hunting for Salmon

Introduction

Suddenly, a massive roil shattered the calm, tranquil, gray-green water as coho salmon darted into frantically leaping, spraying schools of herring. There was no escape, as hovering seagulls with extended beaks grabbed at this multitude of panicked bait fish, further decimating these herded lemmings of the sea.

It was my turn to bring the boat close to the edge of this frantic action while my partner cleared his fly line, quickly false-casting to reach a comfortable

length for a clear cast. In moments, I had the boat at the edge of the roiling action. My partner made one last long false-cast to ensure full control of his fly line, then dropped his herring imitation fly into the melee. Following the cast, he set himself, immediately prepared to quickly strip the fly through the roil, but it was unnecessary. The moment the fly hit the water, he was fast to a silver water-walking coho.

This was not the first fish of the day nor, as it happened, did it become the last, but it was a classic example of the success of a day *hunting* for salmon.

Hunting for salmon is not a new concept. Almost without exception, anglers who go salmon fishing in open water are continually using various visual hunting clues throughout the day as they search for these highly active sports fish. These visual clues include bird concentrations, tide lines and leaping salmon. The skills anglers develop and how they interpret the various clues presented will invariably determine the success they will achieve during each trip. It is the chase and the reward of salmon in the creel that will determine the extent to which each angler pursues his sport.

Active anglers are true examples of the hunter-gatherer dormant within us all. It is our genetic heritage that permits us to draw upon these age-old skills of stalking and successfully interpreting outdoor signals.

For the angler who wishes more success or the sheer pleasure of experiencing and participating in this new fishery—saltwater salmon fly fishing—there are some considerations. The first assumes the angler has a desire to learn each time he ventures out; a crucial element in amassing a base of experiences, thereby enhancing the intuitive sense the angler will heed when fishing. This is one aspect of angling I cannot stress too strongly. It is that intuitive feeling, a *sixth sense* we all feel during a day's angling that tells us the fish are in a specific location. It is the educated guess that results from long observations and many experiences. The angler who accepts this concept and makes a point during every trip to learn new factors, new locations and make new observations will inevitably become the master angler.

A second assumption is that the fly angler who tries saltwater fly fishing for salmon is willing to persist. You may be one of those rare and fortunate anglers with the skills that bring instant success but, for the majority of us, the specialized art of saltwater fly fishing for salmon demands much time and often, many frustrations. For these latter anglers I can assure you patience will provide, success will come, and soon it will be a constant as your skills and knowledge develop.

A third and final assumption is that the angler has the skills required for fly fishing, such as the basic knowledge of knots, sharp hooks and casting, but not necessarily long-distance casting ability.

In an attempt to categorize the basics of hunting for salmon I have developed the following broad categories. While each is crucial, it is their combination that assures success. In no order of priority I would generalize them as follows:

Sea Bird Activity Including Gulls and Auks

Not every day is a fly fishing day! This fact was very clear one day while watching and hearing the bird activity on the water. I had just arrived at a particular up-rising underwater bench where I wanted to anchor and had turned off the motor in preparation to align myself to drop the anchor. Immediately, I was assaulted by the sound of bird activity that comes only after feeding. Various auks were calling to each other in their hoarse, barking call, while others, in pairs, were wing-flapping as they stood up in the water, washing and dusting themselves, all swimming to shore. It was obvious the feasting was over. Intuitively, I had that feeling that the action was over, the *bite* finished, and that I had arrived too late.

After I had anchored and cast a while, the sounds on the waters quieted and it became obvious I would have to hunt elsewhere if I was going to find fish.

The Pacific coast of British Columbia alone has an estimated 17,000 miles of indented shoreline. Include those of Alaska, Washington, Oregon and even northern California and you have infinite salmon locations with countless millions of sea birds. It is an incredibly rich *avifauna,* providing the saltwater salmon fly angler with multiple clues for success during a day's fishing.

Reading the signals of these birds is a major angling skill equal to that of reading the current signals in a stream pool to locate holding areas for trout. Following, I have generalized some sea bird activity clues that should start the saltwater salmon fly fisherman on an exciting search.

Concentrations of Large Gulls in Open Water

Gull concentration can occur at any time, often kilometers from shore. When you motor close with your boat, you will likely notice a flurry of noise and much squabbling among the gulls. Without question, you have spotted a *herring ball* or compacted school of bait fish herded to the surface by predators.

Two conditions usually exist. The first consists of many long-necked loons or other diving ducks in the immediate area. These birds have compacted a bait school and have driven it to the surface, where the gulls are feeding. This particular school is usually stationary and rarely contains feeding salmon.

The second situation with large gulls usually involves a rapidly moving herring ball, being driven by feeding salmon. The salmon have concentrated a school of bait fish which they have either driven to the surface or, more likely, near the surface. Gulls flying above have spotted the flash of the bait fish, chased by the continually prodding salmon and hover to snap up any breaking the surface. A good axiom here could be, "The larger the bait fish the larger the salmon." That is, coho will do this with young herring and needlefish, while chinook will tend to chase the larger jack, two- and three-year-old herring.

Like the gulls, this is opportunistic fishing for the fly fisherman. Wait until the herring are near the surface before casting. If salmon do not strike within moments of your fly striking the water, they have moved on behind the bait school.

A further common situation occurs where large gulls fly high in singles, occasionally power-diving to the surface. This activity usually covers a large area or flat and is the result of salmon chasing and feeding on small, isolated schools of bait fish.

Dip-Diving Hovering Small Gulls

Each sea bird species has its special meaning to the open water salmon fly fisherman. Some are so important they even have local names to signify their relationship to the sport. The small Bonaparte's gull is, without question, the *coho gull*. This common small gull concentrates wherever coho are feeding and is a certain signal the *bite* is on! Along with its cousin, the mew gull, the black-headed Bonaparte's gull will hover, dip and dive over young herring schools being moved to the surface by feeding coho. The mew gull is difficult to distinguish from an immature Bonaparte's gull except the latter has a spot on the side of its head that, once located, makes it easy to identify.

Never underestimate the activity—or lack of activity—of these gulls. While hunting for salmon I have often located a small number of these gulls hovering near a particular section of a kelp bed and it turned out to be the only area producing feeding salmon. Whenever I have seen these gulls on a "loafing bar"—a point of land on the shore—their sheer inactivity is a certain signal the salmon bite is off.

Another sea bird of significance is the small, dark, marbled murrelet. These diving, fish-feeding sea birds are usually inshore or on shallows. They have a low profile in the water and are always in pairs. If separated from each other, their sharp cries carry over great distances and will continue until they are again fishing together. My experience with these birds has shown that wherever these paired birds are found there will be small schools of bait fish, often with feeding salmon.

Many other species of water birds inhabit the coastal waters of the Pacific Northwest. Each has a specific feeding pattern that can provide signals for the hunting salmon fly angler. Seasonal distributions of these birds also provide clues, as they have arrived at that locale to capitalize on bait fish populations during their migrations. Mew and glaucous-winged gulls congregate by the tens of thousands in the spring to feed on herring and their spawn. The Bonaparte's gull arrives in late spring to concentrate on the small herring fry of the year, the feed of choice for coho.

Other sea birds, particularly the auks, are signals

as well for the angler. Most are fish feeders, concentrating on the bait fish on which the salmon feed although a few, such as the ancient murrelet and Cassin's auklet also feed on *euphasiids,* a primary feed of coho and pink blueback salmon. The marbled murrelet and pigeon guillemot are inshore feeders while still others, such as the drab common murre and diminutive ancient murrelet, are distant offshore feeders. I've often followed and used the family flocks of loons and common murres to locate salmon schools while hunting open water in the evening.

"Follow the birds," is an accurate truism for the saltwater fly fishing angler. However, it is imperative for consistent success to become familiar with water bird activity and identification.

Tide Levels, Currents, and Waves

"*Tide* is the rhythmic rise and fall of sea levels, while *tide currents* are the horizontal movements of water associated with the tide." Where the tidal currents are strong, cormorants, loons, murres and gulls will tend to concentrate while diving ducks and auks predominate where currents are weak, as in bays and flats.

Low tides play a key role for the salmon fly fisherman for they will, in consort with salmon and dogfish, concentrate young herring in shallow waters, producing one of those natural phenomena that is the hunting fly fisherman's goal!

I had the following experience during one midsummer low-tide trip that amply demonstrates the importance of this for the saltwater fly fisherman.

A mature bald eagle sitting on the rocks at the south end of Flora Island drew my attention during midmorning. It was a scheduled low tide of 2.3 feet and, as always, I was hunting for those elusive feeding coho. It has been my experience that low tides often draw young herring toward shallow areas, obviously seeking an escape area from feeding salmon and, for this reason, I chose the shallows near the island.

My first run around the southern tip of the island was uneventful except for the chance to view the majesty of that white-headed predator. On the rocks, the usual harbor seals rested, sunning and snorting at each other. A few sport boats were working the outside of the island, but were far from the actual shallows.

In the half-hectare area at the south end of Flora Island I found young herring jammed against the shore. Like the suspended, twisting, turning, curving molecules of a helix, this was the escape pattern for the swimming yearling herring. Throughout this compact mass, dogfish slowly wove an unending, undetermined pattern, breaking the masses into the flowing helix. High dorsal fins and the sharp, knife-like tails of these mud sharks sliced through the mass which, when viewed closer up, showed the occasional quick spurt forward as the dogfish panicked a section of bait and fed on those unable to remain inside the flowing pattern.

While the feeding activity of the sharks was almost mesmerizing in its slow movement, the evidence of salmon was startling! A sharp slap on the water, often followed by a quick glimpse of the deep green back and silver sides of these predators punctuated the massed schools of young herring often followed, in the same location, by another section of roiling water as the salmon struck a second, then a third, time.

The first evidence of salmon feeding activity was a sparkling shower of herring on the surface. This herring shower would move in a particular direction, leaping at the surface as they sought to escape the prodding salmon. Again, a closer examination showed compacted herring at the surface while the salmon traveled below.

It was about half an hour before I realized that single feeding chinook salmon were responsible for the resounding surface boils. A few coho were evident as they surfaced, leaping at the surface and diving down on the panicked herring. Often two, three, or more coho were in evidence but the chinook salmon rarely broke the surface and, if parts of their bodies showed, it was only for an instant as they struck at those herring which had compacted.

The water was clear with the bottom varying in depths between three to eight meters where I anchored to cast. The tide was just reaching the ebb slack and had exposed the many varieties and colors of seaweed growing in this tidal transition zone.

I was fishing the silver tip Silver Thorn fly tied on a Mustad 34011 number two stainless steel hook. My running wet fly line ended with a number eleven shooting head. Even at slack, the tidal current was moving from north to south along the outer side of the island, necessitating an up-current cast to make certain the line would sink sufficiently to place the fly at the correct depth under the compacted herring.

My first strike was a solid take, like a runaway locomotive! No other description fits as well. At the bite of the hook, the chinook salmon headed south toward the deep water in a non-stop run. When the thirty meters of running wet line I had attached to the shooting head zipped through the rod guides, I checked the anchor line to see if I could pull anchor, start the motor and try to chase the fish into the deep water. At the speed the 200 meters of backing was traveling off the reel, I knew this was hopeless. Pulling back on the fish, I applied increasing pressure trying to stop and turn the fish but it was to no avail. Finally, as I watched the circumference of the spool of backing diminish alarmingly, I held back even harder and broke the ten-pound leader tippet.

During the previous year, I had a similar strike from another big spring and have decided a clip-on float attached to my anchor rope is the only solution when I hook one of these fish. They *must* be chased!

After reeling back the line—and this took time—I tied on another ten-pound tippet with another Silver Thorn pattern and began casting once again. This time, a school of coho repeatedly broke the surface just out of casting range, where the bulk of the herring had moved. Showers of herring continued to travel along the surface in various areas in such a way that it appeared continuous. Meanwhile, an occasional resounding splash and surface roil revealed the location of the larger springs. The *helix ribbons* of herring split out, then re-formed, constantly swimming with the steady current flowing south, parallel to the island. Surprisingly, no feeding gulls were evident although a few mature glaucous-winged gulls loafed on rocks near the seals.

I lifted anchor when I realized the herring appeared to be compacting closer to the point of the island, motored to a new location about the distance of a cast from the shore, then dropped the anchor. The herring appeared even further compressed in this location, forming a deep gray-brown cloud that covered the rich yellow-greens of the submerged seaweed.

Just beyond the herring I could see the dark shape of another school of herring. Surface showers seemed focused on the outer edge of these schools, where I centered my casts, hoping to expose the fly as prodding salmon chased the herring closer to shore.

The anticipation was intense for I knew it was only a matter of time before these circumstances occurred and a salmon decided to take my fly.

When the strike did come, it was an instant, water-walking coho, shooting out of the water, surface-rolling and diving repeatedly as I checked the line at my feet for snags. Seals nearby worried me that one would dart in and grab the hooked fish but, surprisingly, not a single seal took a pass at the coho while I played him out.

This silver acrobat's first run took about half of the running line but, like most coho, he chose to fight the fly by jumping and rolling rather than, as had the spring, running away from the boat. Within a few minutes, I had him close to the boat and watched as his struggle panicked and cleared away the compacted herring hiding under the boat.

When the tide flooded sufficiently to scatter the herring, I had boated two silver bright coho and hooked and lost three *locomotives*. It was a memorable trip, proving once again the importance of heeding low tide and its effect on bait fish.

Salmon on the Surface or Leaping

Of all the clues the fly fisherman sees, none pumps more adrenaline into his system than the sight of a leaping salmon; that flash of silver, close by or on the horizon, draws an exclamation of sheer delight and challenge.

Biologists have categorized salmon clearing the surface into leaping, breaching and porpoising but, to the angler, no technical term can classify the feeling he has when a salmon leaps nearby. Forgotten are the sore casting arms; ignored are the stiff backs; the blood roars and the heart thumps against the chest. Hunting in his boat, wading along a beach, or at anchor, if a salmon leaps nearby, the fly fisherman's skills suddenly reach a fine-honed edge.

When I spot a leaping salmon, I will immediately motor to that area to check for a school of fish. It is a rare strike that will occur when salmon are leaping but you know they are there! Occasionally, casting to the salmon window—that surface cone common to feeding trout—will produce a strike. I have had it happen enough times to now make a habit of casting to that surface circle whenever I see a leaping fish.

Bait Schools and Bait Fish Activity

No other natural activity excites the seasoned salmon angler more than watching a herring ball on the surface being worked by salmon! For the saltwater salmon fly fisherman, this natural activity provides one of the most visual opportunities for certain success. Motoring immediately to within casting distance of this flurry of activity and then casting a silver imitation fly into the melee will almost guarantee a strike from a voraciously feeding salmon.

Visualizing the activity beneath the surface helps to understand why this means almost instant success. A herring ball is a packed school of herring forced to the surface by feeding salmon or sea birds. Using the only survival tool available to them—the confusion and safety of numbers—the herring will compact among themselves as feeding salmon or sea birds swim around them. The prodding predators force the bait fish closer and closer together, flushing singles from the school and snapping them up.

I prefer the poetic vision whenever I see this activity. In this view, like a pack of wolves chasing a herd of caribou, the pack cuts a smaller group from the main herd. Similarly, feeding coho will cut out a smaller school of herring who, by instinct, will school close together for safety. Once the coho isolate this smaller school, they again dash toward the bait fish, prodding them to isolate singles, which they can attack while moving the school toward the surface.

When the bait fish near the surface, they attract the attention of searching gulls, who will hover over the herring ball, giving the angler the one surface clue that feeding salmon are in the area. Surfacing effectively traps the herring, surrounded by the coho, who will dart into the school, grabbing those unable to escape and crippling others as they dash by. The coho quickly snap up these stunned and crippled herring and herein lies the secret for the fly fisherman—a feeding-frenzied salmon will grab a cast silver fly landing in the midst of this melee!

We freely admit that we know less about the vast oceans of this planet than we do about the surface of the moon. While our limited knowledge of the north Pacific salmon odyssey grows with each day and season, we are fortunate that Pacific salmon do have basic migration routes close to the continental shelf and that they do travel even closer to the shoreline at predictable times each year. We are also aware that protected saltwater areas such as the Strait of Georgia, Puget Sound and the numerous inlets along the coast do hold salmon for varying periods of time such that they become accessible to the sports angler. Observing the various natural elements in the salmon's inshore habitat gives the fly fisherman the opportunity to angle for these sporting trophy fish at a time when they are nearing their natal waters and are close to maximum growth. However, as all anglers know, fish are not predictable. We don't know why they would leave a particularly rich feeding area or how they can return to their natal stream after a two- to five-year odyssey and no one has yet arrived at the definitive answer that accounts for all the variables in this incredible natural phenomenon, yet, every year adds a new element and the jigsaw web becomes more clear.

Saltwater fly fishing is still in its pioneer infancy and only if the angler uses his *hunting instinct,* is it possible to achieve success consistently.

A Key to Salmon Hunting Conditions

The following key represents common saltwater opportunities open to fly fishers. Exceptions always occur and the angler should be ready for these. However, in the following situations it has been my experience that these are the best choices.

	Anchor	Opportunistic Chase Casting	Continue Hunting
Scattered sea birds			x
Concentrated large gulls			x
Large gulls hovering on moving bait school		x	
High-flying, power-diving large gulls	x	x	
Small dip-diving gulls, on open water		x	
Small dip-diving gulls, near kelp	x		
Few surface birds seen			x
Salmon jumping, open water			x
Salmon jumping, inshore	x		
Salmon surface feeding activity, inshore	x		
Salmon surface feeding activity, open water		x	
Herring schools in streams, not compacted			x
Low tide; compact shore bait fish	x		

2

The Fish!
Family Salmonidae
Genus *Oncorhynchus*

Introduction

My many experiences with this glorious fish genus likely parallel those of the reader. A few stand out more than others, with a very few indelibly etched in my mind. Each species has given me a world of wonder and presents an unforgettable challenge.

My first introduction to the full power of ocean salmon hooked on a fly came with a late October visit

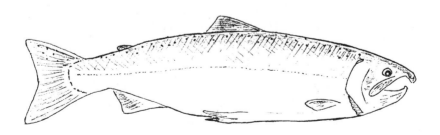

to the estuary of Black Creek bordering British Columbia's Miracle Beach Provincial Park in the late 1960s. I was there to fish for the fall sea-run cutthroat trout, referred to locally as the *Harvest Trout*. Rod Haig-Brown had mentioned this stream during one of our many steelhead discussions and I had it reinforced the previous winter when I watched Dr. Phil Power and his wife, Ivy, catch and tag steelhead under the Park bridge. Stories of these Harvest or, *Tinsel* trout, along with the mysterious stories of wild hook-nosed northern coho caught fly fishing had sent me to the open beach. My first salmon hooked on a Micky Fin fly in the salt water came at the estuary of this small stream while I was covering several smaller leaping jack coho. When the fish struck, it darted between the legs of my partner's waders and, while he goose-stepped to escape, it shot out into the open bay. The sheer power of this three-kilogram fish was astounding as I found it almost impossible to finally reel in the backing I had fortunately placed on the reel. It was not a large fish as coho salmon go but, at last it floated over on its side and I guided it onto the cobblestone beach. It was the first and it proved that a fly fishing saltwater fishery for Pacific salmon was possible. It was a moment to remember and forever dissipated those voices who not only said it couldn't be done, but also indicated that anyone who tried to catch a salmon fly fishing in salt water was somehow addled.

Today, these same beaches, north and south of the mouth of Black Creek, Saratoga and Miracle Beach, annually host numerous fly fisherman from all over the Pacific Northwest. They come to sample a unique fly fishery, one that provides those extremely powerful hook-nosed northern coho in ankle-deep salt water.

My next memorable experience saltwater fly fishing for Pacific salmon came late one July on the beaches north of the Adam and Eve River in Johnstone Strait. My partner and I had canoed along the beach to reach the river mouth, hoping to find the reported schools of pink salmon. They were there and on a cast from the bow of the canoe my partner hooked a lively fish. Beaching the canoe, I steadied the vessel while my partner stepped out. At that moment, an orca surfaced within meters of the canoe, slashing through the salmon school we had just left. It was a moment to remember!

My infatuation with steelhead led me to several rivers during autumn when salmon runs practically choked the pools. One afternoon, using a blue and silver fly, I hooked and released four of the five salmon species, a coho, a chinook, a chum and a pink, all on the same fly, one after the other. A first of firsts and another afternoon to remember!

Locations and timing of salmon runs are, naturally, crucial for Pacific salmon fly fishing success. These will come after much hunting but need to be supplemented with a basic knowledge of the fish. Throughout the Pacific Northwest from California to Alaska, homing salmon enter their natal streams at different times according to weather and species. A compendium of scientific river information is necessary to determine what dates are most productive for which streams. I refer the reader to the many excellent scientific journals, local fisheries officers, or, government publications to obtain that base of knowledge necessary for local success.

Following is some core information, supplemented

with some personal experience that should help in your quest for these magnificent sporting fish.

On the Pacific Ocean the family Salmonidae is composed of the genus *Salmo,* the Atlantic salmon; the genus *Salvelinus,* the brook trout and char; and the genus *Oncorhynchus,* the six salmon species and, recently added, the steelhead trout.

The most generally accepted theory is that the Atlantic salmon and the other members of the family Salmonidae shared a common ancestor until about two million years ago, when the Arctic polar ice sheet separated them.

In the rich seas of the north Pacific the genus oncorhynchus evolved with its six distinct species. Only one, the Cherry salmon *(O. masou),* did not populate the waters of the Pacific Northwest, limiting itself instead, to the Japanese islands and the nearby Asian mainland.

In modern times the five salmon species of oncorhynchus populating the waters of North America all exhibit a similar life odyssey. Reaching the ocean after the fry/smolt stage, the rising spring and summer water temperatures move the fish northward. Complementing this migration are the north Pacific ocean currents, which flow counter-clockwise along the continental shelf. These currents, truly mighty ocean rivers, teem with life, from microscopic plants to *zooplankton* and upward through the oceanic predator prey cycle, culminating in salmon, sharks and sea mammals. It is an ideal environment, a great and vast nursery for the ever-growing, uncountable millions of salmon.

Triggers, such as temperature, light, food availability, genetic factors and others, turn this mass migration in the waters of the north Pacific Ocean, starting these salmon on their return journey along the continental shelf of North America as they return to their natal stream. It is on their return journey, when they tend to travel close to shore, that they are accessible to the saltwater fly fisherman.

Coho Salmon *(Oncorhynchus kisutch)*
Silver, Blueback, Hook-Nose, Northern, the Prince of Salmon

Determined to relax from the adrenaline high I'd been on for the past two hours, I finally sat down and poured a cup of coffee. I had anchored in six feet of water at the north end of Francisco Point inside a kelp bed extending in one large crescent around the point. The coho had been there when I arrived at 7:00 A.M., feeding on the young herring they had forced into the shallows.

I had a good morning, hooking seven powerful coho and boating three and watched showering herring in small groups leap for safety from another inshore feeding coho. I had been fishing on an ebbing tide, concentrating on the edge of a large flat-topped boulder a little larger than my boat where the herring seemed to concentrate and draw the coho. Again, another crescent of herring made the urge to cast overwhelming but I also knew a good cup of coffee would, in the end, give me that needed energy required for another bout with these exciting fish.

I had casually left my rod lying at the bottom of the boat with the pink Silver Thorn pattern dangling on the surface. The rod suddenly bounced on the bottom of the boat as the reel gave a scream! Coffee went one way and the cup another as I frantically grabbed for the rod. Another coho, this time a *reel-burner* who, having hooked himself when he struck the dappling fly, headed for deeper water, slicing through the kelp fronds and beyond, finally to be lost when I thumbed back on the reel in an attempt to hold him.

This was mid-July, with a strong high pressure

ridge settled in over the Pacific Northwest. Tides were falling lower each day and I was to have a glorious week before the low tide began to climb. Not surprising, at tide change the action slowed, then stopped, but as I was to experience, would pick up again the following day. The concentration of coho was the result of a thick surface plankton bloom, darkening the water so the herring were difficult to find except near the shore where tide movement kept the water clear. This was the third consecutive year that I was to experience that supreme shallow-water salmon fly fishing during the summer full moon.

Throughout these fabulous days, small young coho were evident and, on occasion, I watched their successful attack on the forever-harassed herring. These young coho were only a few months from their natal streams but they would be the mature fish of next summer. The attack was fascinating and showed the patient stalking ability of these primary predators of the sea.

Under the boat, the young herring were schooling from tight, compact groups to loose individuals, keeping a few centimeters between themselves. The young coho, about twenty centimeters long, were slowly swimming under the school, moving along the school's length then back again, obviously ready to pounce on any single herring swimming above them. Without apparent warning, a salmon would dart upwards, snapping at a specific herring, who seemed rarely to manage an escape from this sudden strike. The salmon invariably snapped the herring in the middle of its body, resulting in a small cloud of minute scales. Stunned, the herring drifted while the salmon, like a great blue heron, turned the bait fish and swallowed it head first.

I like to call the coho the Prince of Salmon. He is ⋅ the silver flashy showboat, the leaper *(salar)* of this unique race of ocean-going sport fish. Fortunately, the coho salmon is a creek fish and the adoption of these miniature waterways as parks and symbols of wildlife and nature help assure his survival into the next century. If Vancouver Island has over 2,000 named creeks and river tributaries, I know the Pacific Northwest has at least 200,000 similarly named small watersheds, all with runs of these superb fighting salmon.

For the Prince of Salmon, rivers are the highways leading through coastal mountains to inland creeks and small streams. These small watersheds are the homes, the nurseries for this striking member of the Salmonid family.

Throughout the Pacific Northwest, the coho has a consistent life history. Spawned in November or December, he remains in his natal watershed for a period of slightly over one year, migrating to the ocean in April and May of his second year. He will spend about a year and a half in salt water and return in late summer and fall to spawn. A number of precocious small males will return to spawn after only one season in salt water. It is rare for a coho to spend three years in salt water.

In their nursery creeks the coho fry are brown-backed with heavy parr marks and bright orange fins. They tend to concentrate in shaded pools avoiding the fast water riffle zones and feed primarily on surface insects and *biomass* materials.

Unfortunately, because they favor small streams, coho are the victims of irresponsible land development. Their numbers have decreased with urban sprawl and will continue to do so unless there is a continual vigilance for their protection. A land stewardship ethic must be the future for our coho salmon. It must be one that corrects drastic urbanization and outlaws all *channelization* along these sensitive salmon nurseries. Organized anglers and environmentalists have continually flagged this issue since the turn of the century, yet governments at all levels are slow to heed the obvious. Fortunately, in the past decade, the public has taken up the call of organized anglers with the result that we now see the beginnings of federal, regional, local and even community regulations to protect these nurseries.

My memories with the Prince are many! All evoke nostalgic pictures of silver bright, dashing, powerful tail-walking salmon! From April through October, for seven long months, he is accessible in the many waters and fjords of the Pacific Northwest, a tantalizing trophy ready and waiting for the saltwater fly fisher!

Pink Salmon *(Oncorhynchus gorbuscha)*
Humpy, Humpback

Late in July, I was fast-stripping a golden fly at the estuary of the Oyster River, covering what I first thought was a surface rise of a good sea-run cutthroat trout, but there was no strike! The next time the fish surfaced with just its dorsal fin showing, I realized that I was looking at a pink salmon, one of the first to return to this magnificent Vancouver Island river, just beginning to recover from past disastrous clear-cut logging upstream.

Checking my fly fishing vest I frantically searched for a fly box with any pink fly. Unfortunately, as all fly fishermen practice the art of *cleaning* at least once a year, I realized that earlier that week I had finally, but thoroughly, cleaned out my vest to take out a few pounds of extras that always dragged me down. The "Pink Eve Fly Box," which I always carried with me when I am estuary fishing, was one of the victims of that dreaded cleaning and now sat in a drawer at home.

After several minutes of frustrated panic, I realized it was no use; my thoroughness was to be my downfall that day. Rationalizing that the pinks would likely be here tomorrow, I composed myself, resigned to the fact that the pinks would have to wait another day.

Sitting on the sand with a beach log at my back, I watched first one and then another pink rise in the shallows of the low tide estuary. As I watched, I thought back on the previous week when I was sitting on a similar beach, also at low tide, watching other

36

pink salmon as they moved upstream in their natal river.

With a surge, the pink salmon broke water, leaping a good meter in the air as it tried to shake loose the small fly in its mouth. As it hit the water, the rod suddenly snapped straight and I realized he was gone! As I reeled in the line to check the hook, I heard a muffled bark from the beach behind me and looked at my four-legged fishing partner, who was looking upstream at a riffle area a good hundred meters upstream where two blacktail deer were gingerly high-stepping as they slowly picked their way across the stream. The sun had not yet breached the trees in the pool I was fishing but, in the riffle area, an old back channel of river bed had cut a swath through the alders, leaving the deer flooded in early-morning sunlight. It seemed fitting at that moment that the majestic bald eagle who held this stretch of river as his territory, whistled from his high perch atop a douglas fir to alert the intruders that they were trespassing.

I reeled in the remaining fly line and checked the silver bodied Pink Eve streamer fly. No wind knots had formed on the leader and the hook still ran straight and true from the eye knot. I positioned myself again in the waist-deep water and began to false-cast out over the tidal pool until I had reached the brush line on the far bank. At that point, I laid the line on the water, about thirty degrees downstream. When it gently caressed the water surface, the number eight weight forward sink-tip fly line, with its twenty feet of fast-sinking deep green line quickly disappeared, leaving the trailing leaf-green floating line to mark its swing downstream.

I began a very slow, almost nymph-like retrieve, feeling delicately for the pause when a salmon mouthed the fly. I could feel the occasional tick as the line brushed over the rocks on the river bottom. When the line had completed its full sixty degree sweep and was streaming straight downstream, I paused in my retrieve to see if a fish would take as the fly undulated in the current.

At the first strip of line I felt a slight tug and slowly lifted the rod tip to strike. I felt the thump-thump on the end of the line as the fish shook his head to dislodge the fly, then the sudden strike as the fish panicked, turned, and dashed downstream. In a matter of seconds, the loose line from the retrieve tightened and I leaned backward, arcing the fly rod to the flash-ing pink salmon.

His first run took me to the last few winds of the fly line sitting on the braided backing, then he shot upstream while I frantically reeled the slack line back to the reel. In this upstream run, the line sliced through the water leaving a wake on the surface and a small *rooster-tail* where air and water met at the line. The sunken fly line held a great belly in the water, holding the hook firm until I caught up to the fish with the reel.

He leaped once, twice, then a third time before again streaking downstream but this time I was in control! He halted downstream, shaking his head, then arched his body against the current as he slowly drifted into the main river to use the force of the water and his body to pull against the leader. Soon he was on the far side of the stream, pulling the line until he felt the gravel bed below. With a quick turn, he headed back to the main current.

What began then was a repeat of what had hap-pened all afternoon and evening of the previous day. As I reeled in the line the fish would make short dashes, circle me as I stood waist-deep in the water then, ever so slowly, lay over on his side. I would reach down and, carefully balancing the weight of the fish while he lay in the water, ease the barbless hook out with my right hand.

I held this fish for a moment as I felt his weight, marveled at his silver beauty, then lowered him into the pool, where he—slowly at first then, with the realization of freedom, with a burst of speed—headed back to the depths of the pool. In the very clear late summer water, I watched him move to the slot in the pool and disappear in the salmon carpet of gray shadows covering that deep run and gravel slope of the estuary's Pink Pool.

The wind gusted at that moment, blowing upstream from the estuary flats at the narrows of Johnstone Strait and left a heavy ripple on the pool, blotting the patches of gray that were a fresh run of pink salmon returning to this, their home river, for that final and major purpose of their life. This was one of many memories I have of this feisty little fish.

The pink salmon has the simplest and least complicated life history of all Pacific salmons. When the eggs hatch, the tiny fish are already silver sided without the spots or parr marks of the other salmon. They migrate immediately to the sea and spend the approximate year and a half before their return wandering in the north Pacific, then traveling to the estuary of their home river to spawn in September or October. Most mature pinks weigh a little under and over four pounds, with an exceptional fish weighing up to ten pounds.

Prior to the Canadian government's hatchery programs of the Salmonid Enhancement Program, pink salmon were rare in the Strait of Georgia streams south of Johnstone Strait except for the Fraser River. The impression was then that the larger runs were during odd years with limited exceptions. The introduction of these fish to many Strait of Georgia streams has now provided both odd and even year runs of large numbers of these fish. For the fly fisherman this is a blessing and has created a new sports fishery. I will be discussing this in detail in the chapter on beach fly fishing.

Now, back to that stream in Johnstone Strait, the estuary that taught me many techniques for saltwater salmon fly fishing and provided me with many memorable experiences with this exciting salmon.

On one trip my partner and I had traveled on a recently created logging road to a logging company's dry-land sort at the stream's estuary. This provided access to the beach. Here we had unloaded my canoe and stowed our gear for the kilometer paddle along the beach to the river's mouth. The anticipation of trying my now perfected Pink Eve fly, which had been so successful in previous years heightened that trip's excitement.

When all was ready we launched the canoe, allowing our two Brittany spaniels to run along the beach as we paddled to the river mouth. It was still early morning and an ebbing tide had smoothed the waters of Johnstone Strait, permitting an easy paddle. We knew that, at the slack, the prevailing strong winds of the strait would whitecap the waters we now traveled but, for the moment, all was calm. The sheer wildness of this location was intoxicating but there was to be more.

We were half way to the river mouth when we saw our first salmon leaping a few hundred meters from shore. From the leap, we were certain it was a coho.

Closer to the river mouth we spotted several porpoising, dolphining salmon we knew were pinks, so we quickly prepared and readied the fly rods. As we drew near, my partner made a few false-casts, then gently dropped a Pink Eve fly near the school. Almost instantly there was a strike from a good fish and, surprisingly, a coho leaped. The fighting position was awkward for my partner so I eased the canoe toward the beach. A few good strokes grounded the bow and my partner stumbled out. The fish was now catapulting close to shore, then lay on its side while my partner slid it onto the beach.

At that exact moment we both became aware of a sudden *whooshing* sound near the shore. A pair of orcas were roiling the waters where the canoe had floated when the coho struck. The sound and the immense dorsal fins showing as the whales surfaced were stunning! They were so close even a false-cast would have covered those immense fins.

We stood in awe as we watched the black and white mammals disappear, then reappear, only to disappear once again. The waters surrounding them swirled with frothing currents as the whales twisted and turned, slashing at the school of pink salmon.

Suddenly, it was over and the waters calmed. A hundred meters farther up the beach the whales surfaced once again, this time in unison as they moved up the strait in search of more salmon. Farther out in the water, an immense, curving dorsal fin showed on the surface as the bull of this pod cruised through the strait. A second, then a third pair appeared in the immediate area during the next few minutes, then another pair came parallel to the beach toward the river mouth. We beached the canoe very close by and noticed two dark, murky shapes, this time in the shallows. Schools of salmon darted upstream in the river, torpedoing through the shallows of the beach. We watched this new pair of whales froth and roil the waters in a frenzy of water sounds until they too, disappeared.

It was obvious that what we had witnessed was a feeding pod of orcas. They had teamed in pairs and were searching for the schools of salmon abounding in the strait in this late summer of the year. It was a rare opportunity, etched forever in our minds.

Most small coastal streams have a small tidal flat at their estuary, affected twice a day by the flood and ebb of the tide, which can often reach a depth of five meters. The stream course through this tidal flat varies with each watershed but there is always a final pool affected by the tide. I have affectionately dubbed these *Pink Pools,* as they will often hold the upstream migrating salmon while they acclimatize to the fresh water of their home stream.

For the fly fisherman, these are the ultimate classroom, providing an opportunity for experimenting with all manner of tackle and for perfecting those special saltwater fly patterns which ensure success and confidence in open salt water.

Fish newly arrived at the pool greet the angler with porpoise rolls on the surface and occasional wild leaps. Periodically, a silver flash shows in the midst of the gray salmon carpet as a fish turns on its side, showing the brilliant silver that attracts so many predators. In the ways of fish these are mannerisms for the adjustment to a freshwater environment after their year and a half in the salt water of the Pacific Ocean. The wild leaps and river bottom flashes are likely attempts to rid themselves of the sea lice clinging to their bodies, concentrated at the base of the anal fin. The porpoising is likely a way of adjusting to fresh water and the environment of a constraining stream. If recent scientific hypothesis is correct, it also has to do with the seeking of clues recalled in *reverse order sequential imprinting.*

My memories of this particular Johnstone Strait Pink Pool were that it was a classic fly fisherman's run, providing opportunities for virtually every casting and retrieving method. It was more a run than a pool, typical of the lower reaches of most smaller Pacific coastal streams. High winter floods had shifted the river bed, leaving three large alder trees on the beaches behind my casting location but far enough away not to interfere with my back cast. On the high tides this gravel beach flooded through to the old river channel, creating a lake-like pool about two hundred meters wide. At all other times however, the river was about fifteen meters wide.

The Pink Pool begins a few meters above a fallen alder, two-thirds of the way upstream on the far bank, below a shelf of calf-deep riffles. The main current stays on the far side of the pool, running over a sloping gravel area extending about five meters from the far bank, below the overhanging green belt. On the open side from my location, a sandy, small-gravel bottom gently sloped to meet the heavier gravel from the far side. There is a major holding water for the salmon where the gravel meets in a deep groove in the river bed about forty-five to seventy meters in length.

Below this area and, for most of the remainder of the pool, the river bottom was like a dish, running over heavy gravel from either side. In this section of the Pink Pool the water flowed equally fast and was hip-deep. In the deep groove area however, the water was at least three meters deep, with a fast flow on the gravel side and a slow flow on the sand side. The gray shadows, the salmon carpet sharpened with my Polaroid glasses, showed continually in the deep run to the fallen alder and down midstream almost to the tailout of the pool.

It was just above this midstream point that I positioned myself. Here, I could lay my fly directly across the stream, aiming it to land close to the small weather-worn tree trunk that butted against the far bank. As the fly began its swing through this faster water, the main body of the floating sink-tip line lay on the slack portion of the pool, accentuating the fly's swing. At this point I would begin a slow but definite fifteen to twenty centimeter strip of the fly line through my right index finger. The strike, when it came, would halt the line and a quick strip with a corresponding rod lift would set the hook. Often, the fish came toward me with the strike, forcing me to back-step, lift the rod and rapidly strip in line just to catch up to the fish. When I did, the salmon would turn, searing the slack line through my finger as he raced to the tailout of the pool and I had him to the reel.

Standing from my midstream point I would alternate my casts, aiming first to the top of the fallen weather-worn tree trunk with my fly, then cast to its midpoint about ten degrees downstream. Then, I would cast to its tip about thirty degrees downstream. This method covered different fish with each retrieve and has proved itself many times since as an effective casting technique. When there was a pause in the action, I would move downstream a few steps, continuing the same pattern until I had covered the whole pool.

On this trip, the salmon appeared highly selective

with the flies I was using. The only successful flies were silver bodies with some pink on them.

Pink salmon have a relatively soft mouth, almost like a whitefish or a grayling, with the result that all strikes must be slow but firm. Too much pressure during the fight will tear the hook from their mouths as I have experienced many times.

To angle for these spunky salmonids is a fly fisherman's dream. I have been fortunate to know of several pink salmon rivers and I know my search will never end for this spunky Pacific coast salmon!

Chinook *(Oncorhynchus tschawytscha)*
Spring, King, Tyee

I have had many memorable fly fishing experiences with this powerhouse, this racehorse, this *King* of the Pacific salmon family—the chinook. The greatest appeal has been the unknown; when I hook a chinook, I am never certain just how large it might be!

The following experience with one particular fish highlights one of many memories I hold for this noble salmon.

I had anchored at an underwater pinnacle and, for two hours, had not had a single strike. This was not an uncommon experience fly fishing for salmon but what made this one unique was the fact that the previous day I had outstanding fly fishing at the same time and place, steadily hooking and releasing coho and jack springs, but today was a blank; zilch, zippo, *zero!*

At the boat ramp I had several conversations with other salmon anglers who had also had a highly successful previous day and were launching their boats in a steady flotilla in anticipation of another day of success. Many of the anglers were very interested in the concept of salmon fly fishing and some had even come prepared with bucktails after watching my antics the previous day. Alas, the salmon had moved and our day was blanked until...

It's an understatement to say I was obvious, anchored in an area with many salmon anglers trolling or drift-fishing the same waters. Standing on the fly fishing platform in the bow of my Boston whaler, I had anchored near a bait school in the calm water. In my open boat, in the open waters at least a mile from shore, I know I became the focus of several conversations. It is amazing how the human voice carries long distances over calm waters. Many of the conversations, easily overheard because they were speaking over the noise of their running outboards, were those of curiosity and interest in the fly fishing possibilities they might experience. Many of the salmon fishermen were trout fly fishermen but had not thought to try their fly fishing skills on salt water. One particular pair of anglers repeatedly trolled past my boat, each time flooding me with questions: "How do you retrieve?" "What fly lines are you using?" "How do you know when you are in salmon fishing waters?" and the most common question, "What fly patterns do you use?" During one of these staccato question periods, a most obliging nine kilogram chinook salmon answered.

I had just cast my fly when the anglers trolled by and, as if on cue, it was on their question of retrieve that the chinook took my fly. The flurry of action immediately following the strike startled everyone. The hook must have hit a sensitive nerve, for the salmon exploded behind my boat within yards of theirs, leaping a good three meters in the air, landing on its side with a terrific *slap*. He repeated this once, twice, then once again while I repeatedly bowed to this magnificent nine kilogram chinook and watched the loose fly line as it streamed, unchecked, through the rod guides. In retrospect, I am certain it was due to his initial explosive surface activity, uncommon for springs, that I was able to finally bring him to the boat in spite of being anchored.

When I hooked the fish, there must have been at least seven sport boats trolling or drift-fishing nearby. The sportsmanship of these anglers was of the highest caliber immediately on sight of my high-flying salmon. They all swung away from my boat, some speeding up to give me lots of clearance with this trophy fly-caught fish.

After the initial surface leaps, the salmon did a complete circle of my boat, swinging to the left each time I applied pressure. Once again he did the unchinook thing of repeatedly leaping and breaching the surface at almost the same location I'd hooked him, but that was to be the last surface action for he then settled into a predictable chinook fight with long, long runs and much head-shaking.

On one of these runs, when it seemed he would take all my backing, a sport boat motored alongside and offered to take me off my anchored boat to chase the fish. His concern and help were an admirable sportsman's offer, giving up his own fishing to assist me when a bite appeared to be imminent. Had the fish continued his power run, I would have taken his offer but declined when I felt the fish slowing. To that sportsman's credit, he stayed near me throughout the fight, ready with his service.

This big chinook also applied all the tricks guaranteed to make your heart stop. On numerous occasions, when he was fifty or more meters away, he would surface, open his mouth and violently shake his head. With no resistance on the surface, I watched the fly flip back and forth on the side of his mouth, each time visualizing it simply popping free. He would sound several times, then simply sit on or near the bottom, doing corkscrew rolls that usually free the hook, due to the pull of the line wrapped around his body. This time, he was unable to free this particular 4/0 Silver Thorn fly.

When I finally felt I had him, he would lie on the surface, facing away from the boat and forcing me to drag him along the surface and still, the fly held. When I did eventually get him in the net, there was a hole in his lip where the hook had held him.

When the struggle was over, this particular salmon epitomized all the thrills and skills associated with saltwater salmon fly fishing. It also reinforced a dimension I had experienced on other occasions—the true sportsmanship exhibited by most salmon anglers.

I mentioned earlier that one of the appeals of fly fishing for chinooks is the unknown associated when a fish is first hooked. Jack springs, those smaller one- and two-kilogram chinook, are particularly active on the end of a fly line. Their struggle is often non-stop, even when finally brought to the boat for release. When fishing in herring, as the following experience shows, you can never be certain which, or what, you have hooked.

Hornby Island is one of many Gulf Islands situated in the Strait of Georgia. Like all the Gulf Islands, it has a Mediterranean climate, since it lies in the rain shadow of Vancouver Island. Approaching northwest Pacific storms vent their fury on the Vancouver Island mountain ranges, then absorb moisture in a Mediterranean manner as they pass over the Strait of Georgia and drop it on the high mainland coastal mountains. This drying effect on the Gulf islands creates dry land conditions, including grass and rock areas with desert prickly pear cactus. It is a haven for nesting birds and for the fly fisherman.

Weather conditions are usually favorable during the summer months and only strong southeast winds hinder the movement of the boating angler. This particular day, I finally anchored on the flats at Nash Banks after having hunted for salmon on the south end of the island.

I watched the big dogfish with their slow, seemingly purposeless cruising as I retrieved the fly through the helix swirls of herring. As one of these particularly large mud sharks came near the surface, I paused in my stripping to watch how he cornered a small school of herring and then, while on the surface, slashed at these panicked bait fish, twisting and turning to keep the mass together so he could lift his snout and feed into the school.

As I began my strip retrieve, I immediately felt the solid take of a heavy fish. Lifting the tip, I set the hook and prepared for the panicked first dash I had experienced with the feeding jack springs in this area but, instead, there was an almost rhythmic head-shaking as the fish sought to tear the fly out of its mouth. Instead of a head shake and dash, the fish came closer and closer to the boat as I stripped in line. In moments, the herring school parted, revealing a large dogfish hooked on my fly. This was not the first time I have hooked these predators with the fly, but dogfish and jack springs had alternately punctuated this day. The only difference in their struggle came after the initial strike. The jack springs would make mad dashes to safety, with long runs then numerous head shakes, twisting and rolling before, once again, making a dash for freedom. The dogfish, on the other hand, never stopped head-shaking, rolling and twisting.

When fly fishing in the deeper water for chinooks, I have often hooked other fin fish as well. Rockfish will take the fly regularly, particularly when I am fishing deep along rocky outcrops or reefs. They are spunky fish on a fly but, like the small-mouth bass, they cease struggling once the first tussle has turned them.

Chinook salmon are the noble kings of the Pacific salmon family. Their life history is, fortunately, highly complicated. The variables within each race will assure their survival, providing man or natural disaster does not eliminate their home stream. Unlike the Princes of the Pacific salmon family—the coho—chinook salmon will reach immense sizes, often in the twenty plus kilogram range, making them a magnificent trophy fish. Their variation in size is a result of their longer life history—up to nine years—and their longer growth period in salt water—up to seven years.

It has been my experience that fly fishers hunting for chinook do so secondary to coho, which tend to be more surface-oriented in their feeding patterns, making them easier to locate. However, as I have related earlier, I have found chinook feeding in the same area as coho on numerous occasions.

Chinook also seem to be single feeders or loners when feeding near the surface. It is rare to have two chinook hooked from the same boat as a double, while this is not uncommon with coho, where it is important to keep fishing while your partner is playing a fish, since the struggling action will draw other coho to the area who will quickly snap up your fly.

The chinook is the loner, the single hunter who presents the challenge of fast waters, windswept lonely surroundings and incredible power for the fly fisherman. When hooked, this king of the salmonids can either be a scrappy jack, a bright spring or an incredible tyee; you will never know until that first run!

3

Fly Casting on Open Salt Water

Introduction

Whenever I saltwater fly fish, I have three basic fly casting outfits set up and ready to use. Since I begin by hunting for salmon, my first outfit is a nine-meter sink-tip line, matching a number eight fly rod, ready for surface feeders. There is instant action when a school of salmon ball the bait fish at the surface but it's fast action. The bait fish ball is moving,

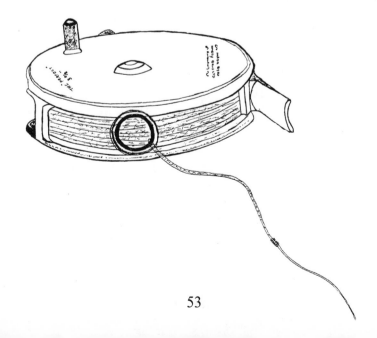

the salmon are moving and my boat must continue to move to keep me within casting range. Usually, just as quickly as they surface, the salmon will sound, only to reappear again on another bait ball and, most times it seems, just beyond casting range, but my success is usually high in these situations, often during a day with many fish hooked.

My second outfit is the workhorse—the system I use most often—once I have located feeding salmon and bait fish, on a shoal or beside a kelp bed, I will anchor and use a prepared number eight, three-meter rod. On the saltwater reel I have placed 200 meters of backing then laid a thirty-meter running extra-fast sinking wet line with a loop at the end. Using this loop system, I attach a variety of extra-fast sinking, ten-meter sinking heads in numbers eight, nine, ten and eleven, depending on the tidal speed of the water. I always begin with the number eleven so I am able to get to the magic salmon-feeding depth of ten meters.

My third outfit is a dry line for opportunistic salmon-surfacing situations. While deep-line fishing, I have often seen salmon cruising along the surface or leaping nearby. I have found that a surface cast ahead of them or where they may have jumped will result in a strike. The dry line outfit allows for a quick surface cast and is productive enough to make it an effective outfit when anchored.

The most common question anglers new to saltwater fly fishing ask is; "Where can I anchor to be certain I am presenting my fly to the best advantage?"

The ocean is a very large body of water but, like all aquatic areas, fish tend to haunt key locations. With lake fishing, it could be a shoal near a drop-off, the plateaued estuary of a feeder stream or a shallow weed bed; all prime locations for feeding trout. Similarly, in the ocean, these favored locations parallel a ledge near the shore adjacent to a deep drop-off, a submerged sand or rock flat or a kelp bed.

One location I have found that provides success on a regular basis during the summer months is at the kelp beds the local anglers know as salmon haunts. These are well-known areas, usually well marked by the flotilla of sport boats fishing nearby. Often, these kelp beds hold summer-long bait fish concentrations of young herring, needlefish or anchovies and will likely produce salmon throughout the summer.

The more productive locations are wherever daily tide changes rapidly ebb and flood along the shoals on which the kelp have anchored. This tide action provides a regular flow of micro-organisms, *(zooplankton)* for the young bait fish which, in turn, concentrates the resident and migrating schools of feeding salmon. The most productive of these fishing holes are near a sheer drop-off or an underwater plateau with a shallow, submerged rock shoal to secure the kelp.

In recent years, I have used a quality depth sounder to locate those specific drop-off areas where I have previously located salmon. I have found that each of these productive areas has several common factors:

First, the area has a regular summer population of young bait fish. Second, each has a kelp bed, changeable each year because kelp is an annual plant, but constant in the vicinity. Third, the kelp is in an area where known populations of salmon migrate. Fourth, these areas are adjacent to a rapid drop-off where it appears the salmon hold in the depths during non-feeding times.

Pacific Northwest salmon movement is an odyssey,

a journey begun in their natal stream when they are but finger size in the fry stage and continues when they travel north, following their entry to the sea as smolts. As young salmon, they migrate even farther north in the waters of the open Pacific Ocean, swinging south with the Aleutian Islands chain and back again, home to their natal stream. Highly complicated factors relating to genetics, weather, moon and tides, photoperiodism, bait fish availability and many other factors trigger this odyssey. It is this information the saltwater salmon fly fisherman must be aware of when he targets the salmon species and locations for his fly fishing. Each species—chinook, pink, sockeye, chum and coho—offers a unique, yet often, common experience. For regular success hunting for salmon, it is necessary to find that daily changing location where migrating or resident schools of salmon are feeding.

It has been my experience, when I have had the opportunity to fish on consecutive days, that I have been able to follow a specific run of salmon, concentrating on those specific sites where they are actively feeding or migrating. Unlike trout, which frequent areas on a regular basis, most salmon in salt water are non-resident to any particular region. This principle difference, combined with tides, predators and bait feed movement, add new dimensions to the fly angler's own odyssey.

Chase Casting

Like skilled horsemen acting as one, the coho out-riders herd the panicking bait fish, taking advantage of the ocean surface to lay a deadly trap. Overhead, a true example of a symbiotic relationship is developing as gulls hover and scream, seeking a prime position for the feast being driven to them.

The bait fish, acting in incredible unison, turn one way, then another, seeking safety in their own numbers while, at the same time, moving, always moving, in search of kelp fronds or others of their kind. However, for this school, numbering in the uncountable thousands, there is no safety as prodding coho dart at the bottom of the school, forcing those above closer to the surface. Above, the pressing gulls force the top members of the school down upon their peers, further compacting this frightened school.

Then, without warning, coho smash through the compact ball of bait fish, grabbing singles as they go and crippling others unable to escape the smash of the predator's tail. Again and again, these efficient salt-water hunters terrify the bait fish while, on the surface, gulls gulp bait fish as fast as their beaks can snap crippling several, quickly snapped up by circling coho.

When the coho are satiated, the main herring school, now numbering in the hundreds, escape the surface gulls who, by this time, are also content to simply swim along above the flash of the bait fish school. Small, splintered bait fish schools swim just beneath the surface, separated from the main school. They swim aimlessly, traveling in all directions in their search for safety only to become the prey of unorganized coho darting out of the depths, snapping up these disoriented stragglers and forcing others to shower the surface, once again attracting those air-bound predators, the gulls.

A cloud of minute scales drifting in the slow current of the saltwater flat marks the trail of this particular carnage. Now fed, the predators dropped back to the depths or flew to their loafing bar. Replete now, but the deadly pattern of predator and prey would begin again later in the day.

I have had many opportunities to witness this shared action of coho and gulls. From June through September this is one of the most dramatic natural events in the salt water of the Pacific Northwest. It seems a never-ending tragedy for the herring, for even when they become larger the chinook salmon use the same hunting technique. Fortunately, the waters along the Pacific continental shelf harbor an immense and uncountable number of herring and other bait fish species, subjected to the same attack by aquatic and aerial predators.

Chase casting to these feeding salmon is an experience every angler will remember for a lifetime. Unlike the satiated salmon, the fly angler satiated with this special fly fishing opportunity is rare, indeed.

Through trial and error I have learned several tips I hope will help to perfect skills for this fascinating and incredibly exciting form of fly fishing.

Surface activity: Motor to it as quickly as possible. Usually, it will only last a matter of seconds but, if you're lucky, it will last long minutes.

Have a line ready: Keep a dry fly line or a short sink tip *always* ready in the boat for just these opportunities. It takes too long to break out a fly casting outfit. Beside my seat I keep a dry fly outfit with false-casting line stripped into a plastic fish tub with the rod hooked on a rack, immediately accessible. Begin to false-cast as you travel to the action, ready to drop a fly into the roiling melee as soon as you get within casting range.

Silver flies: In these fishing circumstances, use a simple, silver-bodied streamer fly that's a close imitation to the bait fish.

Watch their direction: When you get close to the surface activity, turn your motor off and drift parallel to the activity. This is critical! With time, you will learn how close to get before the fish sound. As you are traveling toward them, try to determine the direction in which they are heading so you can steer parallel to that course.

Take turns: This is the most effective method of working these surface bait balls. One angler should steer the boat into a position where the caster will have the most effective chance of hooking a fish. When a fish is hooked, the driver should also cast into the circling coho, as they will often take a fly just as they would a crippled bait fish.

Chase casting is not for the faint of heart! Often, surface boils will occur in many different directions at the same time. When you have made a choice, stick to it but always be prepared to move. Wind action will blow the fly back in your face, every infinitesimal snag in the boat will hook your line, the boat will stop to soon, throwing you forward and the dog will tangle the fly line. In short, it is incredible how many errors you will make in the excitement but, when all goes well, it is impossible to describe how powerful these fish can be and how fully satiated you will feel!

Open Water Anchoring

When I first started fly fishing from an open boat in salt water, I quickly learned that the ocean is like a river—always moving. Anchoring, I found, gave me a chance to present my fly with some confidence, particularly when I learned that, with weighted fly lines, I could easily sink my fly to that magic six- to ten-meter depth, where the salmon range.

Anchoring locations vary with the tides, but one constant is to locate near a kelp bed, but not just any kelp bed. Bait fish are the key and need to be carefully searched for before you drop your anchor.

The most consistent kelp area is usually at the ends of the bed. Here, the young herring, the most dominant feed source for feeding chinook and coho, stray into the deeper, unprotected water, ready to dash back to the safety of the kelp fronds as feeding salmon prod at them. In clear water, you can often watch salmon make short dashes at a bait fish school, or observe them as they cruise under the bait fish, looking for cripples or singles.

Safety lies in numbers for the bait fish and the predator's confusion over a school is akin to the hawk or wolf confronted by a flock or herd—the salmon has difficulty singling out an individual to attack and herein lies one secret of success for the saltwater fly fisherman.

When I have determined where I want to anchor at the end of a kelp bed harboring a major school of bait fish, careful not to spook them, I try to drop my anchor so my boat is holding at the edge of the kelp. Ideally, the herring will stray from the kelp in such a manner that they fan out into the open water beyond

the boat. If feeding salmon are around, the herring will dart back to the security of the kelp, a sure sign I use to determine how long I will stay in a location before searching out another area. No panicking herring means no preying salmon; a simple equation for the fly fisherman.

Should my area be an active one for feeding salmon, I then proceed to cast to the outer edges of the herring school. Salmon strikes, when they occur, happen when the herring dart back to the kelp, leaving my herring imitation fly exposed. I have had the rare opportunity to actually witness this strike in clear water during calm surface days. I can assure you, the sight of a three-kilogram salmon darting in to take your fly creates an unsurpassed adrenaline high!

On one occasion, using a slow short strip of my fly line, I watched a herring school dart under my boat, then spotted three coho staring at my exposed fly. On the next strip of my line, one of the fish darted forward and grabbed the fly. Fortunately, I had seen this before and waited until I felt the slight tug on my line. At other times, I have actually pulled the fly right out of the fish's mouth before it had bit on the fly but, in this particular incident, I had waited and, when I felt the tug, lifted the rod tip to set the hook.

This particular salmon simply came toward me as I began to lift the rod. It wasn't until his head was almost out of the water that he realized something was wrong and darted away, showing me the reaction of salmon from the most common strike when fly fishing in a bait school.

Depending upon tide height and changes, salmon feeding activity and bait fish availability, you may have several successful hours anchored in one location but it has been my experience that you will have to hoist anchor and move to other locations several times during a day's fly fishing. I have often found that one particular school of bait does not produce salmon but another, twenty or more meters away, does. The constant search for that special bait school is one of the variables for which to prepare. Another variable over which you have no control is the distance bait fish will move away from the kelp. Often, kelp-straying herring will move far beyond casting range due to limited salmon preying but, if you're fortunate, the salmon may be under the herring. Then it is a simple matter to attach a heavier fly line, sink under the bait after the cast and retrieve under, then up, through the bait.

Kelp bed anchoring locations give the angler a further chance as a result of the natural behavior of bait fish. As I have indicated, bait fish dart toward the kelp for safety. For this reason, make the majority of your casts out and away from the kelp so that, on the retrieve, your fly behaves as if it, too, is heading for the safety of the kelp. I am certain this direction of retrieve has helped me many times when salmon have appeared dubious about the fly patterns I was presenting to them.

In addition to kelp beds, I have found that sand flats with plateaued shallows and rock pinnacles are effective areas for anchoring. To locate these very specific areas, I make extensive use of charts, my depth sounder and marker buoys.

When I have determined from my charts that there is a shallow plateau in a sand flat, I begin a very slow cruise in the general area, searching for the rise and fall of the sea bed. The magic depth for anchored salmon fly casting appears to be near ten meters. I will start by traveling parallel to some fixed object, to find any water less than this ten-meter depth. Once found, I will begin to drop my buoys, keeping track of the specific depth of where each is placed. In a matter of minutes, using this method, I am able to find where the shallowest water area lies. Once located, I then place the anchor buoy in a specific spot where, when I cast, I am able to use the tide movement to best effect to get my fly line near the bottom. After collecting my scattered buoys, I then move and anchor at the anchor buoy location. On occasion a particular underwater ledge or rock may act as a zone where bait fish and salmon will collect or travel. Marking this in relation to your anchor buoy site is useful for visual casting purposes.

Naturally, should there be a school of bait fish hovering in one particular area of this shallow, that is where I will anchor but in most situations the bait fish will be moving along the flats and it is only a matter of time before they come onto the shallow plateau where you have anchored. This method is particularly effective for those underwater peaks that usually collect bait fish and, of course, feeding salmon.

With this search-and-locate system, the number of locations where bait fish and salmon congregate will astounded you. It is important that you move and search new areas if you do not have success at one particular proven location. I find I will hoist anchor about every half an hour if I have had no strikes in one specific area. Conversely, once I have had a strike in an area, it will take a blasting southeastern storm to move me. This method of hunting for salmon provides a new and exciting dimension to my angling which, I feel, has greatly enhanced my success ratio while saltwater salmon fishing with the fly.

The author with a chinook salmon.

A surface herring ball prodded by slashing coho!

Gulls concentrate on a herring ball feeding voraciously on these herded lemmings of the sea.

At this coho surface action, motor parallel but not too close or the salmon will sound.

Small one kilo (two to three pound) but powerful jack chinook are particularly attracted to the Silver Thorn fly.

Herring, compacted and forced to the surface by prodding coho.

Another skillful angler, a mature bald eagle with a rockfish in his claw.

Killer whales thrashing in shallow waters.

Ralph Shaw sets the hook on a surface coho strike while Elaine Shaw drives the boat.

A pink salmon school, obvious by the leaper, at the estuary of a coastal stream.

The Prince in autumn dress.

A large net is recommended for these large salmon.

Chest waders are a must particularly during ocean swells following a storm. Here, the angler has used the cresting wave to beach his fish.

Ralph Shaw and Roy Taylor show the drift sequence in the hunt-drift-cast method of saltwater fly fishing.

Fluorescent lime green streamer on a silver bodied fly is a most effective color for single leaping coho.

Success will come if the fly fisher is willing to persist! Dr. Martin Lamont holds a sparkling bright blueback coho which took a full afternoon of casting.

A sink-tip fly line gives the angler the greatest control for casting to surfacing salmon.

A leaping pink salmon marks the location of the school for this angler.

Dr. Terry Blasco holds his half of our double, hooked in knee deep water during a flooding tide.

Ethics: here the wading anglers are hampered by the angler in the belly boat who moves in front of them spooking the salmon.

Two hundred meters (yards) show through the reel and is the minimum I would recommend for Pacific salmon fly fishing.

Leaping pink salmon near the end of their Pacific Ocean odyssey.

Silver streamer simplicity succeeds for saltwater salmon.

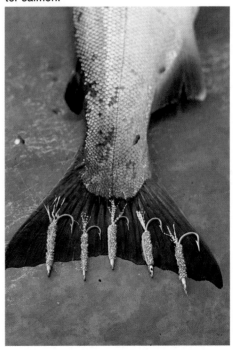

77

An angler's equipment is very personal. Here, the author holds an eight kilo (eighteen pound) chinook taken while casting from his special fly platform at the bow of his Montauk Boston Whaler.

Opposite page inset: Large plastic foam cases hold flies well in a bouncing boat. The visible large selection allows the angler to change sizes to match herring size.

Two summer coho, the quest of the saltwater fly fisher.

A day's catch fly fishing. Note the necessary detachable fighting butt, on this #8 line weight Fenwick outfit.

Hunting salmon anglers, hunting, always hunting for that elusive silver bounty.

Hunt-Drift-Cast for Early Coho

It was to be one of those days! Success was not to be measured by the number of salmon in the boat but, rather, by the pleasure of the day and the knowledge we were to accumulate.

My partner and I cruised south on the flat, smooth waters of the Strait of Georgia, running the motor at a steady 4,000 rpm, the distance-eater that pushed my Boston Whaler at a pleasant thirty miles per hour. We were heading for Collishaw flats at the north end of Hornby Island, an area that, in mid-May, usually held small schools of coho and pink bluebacks.

Blueback is a localized name in the Strait of Georgia for small coho salmon who have not yet reached the two-kilogram size. These are the coho grilse of the previous summer who, this autumn, will travel up their natal stream to spawn. These small salmon, concentrating in large surface schools, become visible in the Strait of Georgia in March. The term "blueback" appears to originate from the deep blue color the dorsal surface takes on after exposure of a dead fish to the air. The color is quite prominent and rarely appears in such intensity with summer coho or pinks.

Blueback schools move north as spring passes, spreading throughout the coast in June. Usually, in early June a major feeding transition occurs when these salmon change their diet from minute pink plankton to bait fish. It is at this time that they have reached that two-kilogram size that earns them the name coho or silver. Often, mixed with these coho bluebacks are pink salmon, identifiable by their small scales and dark tail spots.

Fishing for these small salmon is a controversial

topic among saltwater anglers. Some state that there should not be a season on these immature fish until June or even July, when they have reached coho size. Others state that it is their only opportunity for successful salmon fishing as they feel that the salmon migrate during the summer and are only available when a school moves through their area. Personally, I feel the opportunity to angle should never be lost for sports fishermen. Fisheries could impose tackle restrictions or limits if angling pressure becomes a conservation factor, but the opportunity to fish must never be regulated away!

On this trip, our first sign of fish occurred about three miles from Hornby Island in about seventy-five meters of water. Roiling surface water had arched in a crescent V away from the boat as we passed by—the sign of a surface salmon. Throttling back on the motor, the boat settled back from its high-speed plane and we began to cruise the area, still heading toward the shallower water of the flats but now, alert for other signs of surface-feeding salmon.

Within moments, we spotted a dark patch on the smooth water surface a few hundred meters ahead of the boat. I pointed the boat in that direction while my partner began to get his fly gear assembled. As we neared the area, the flash of silver sides and porpoise-rolling indicated there was a major school of fish feeding. Throttling down even more, I drove the boat near the surface action and cut the motor, allowing us to drift along side. I had stopped the boat about ten meters from a particularly active flock of small gulls, concentrated in an area about the size of a small house, as they continually hovered, then dove into what we could see was a vast smorgasbord of small, surfacing feed, chased there by feeding bluebacks and diving ducks. As we watched, we were soon able to distinguish between the surfacing ducks, concentric circles where the gulls touched the surface and the roils made on the surface from feeding salmon.

As we watched, the area showing surfacing salmon quickly expanded as we were able to distinguish between the surface signs. In moments, we were aware of fish surrounding us, spread over an area the size of a baseball diamond.

This was to be an experimental day and we were well equipped with a variety of lines and a vast array of flies. These early-season salmon were on the surface feeding on *euphasiids* shrimp, known as pink feed in the region—the krill feed of the Arctic responsible for the immense size of plankton-feeding whales.

I had been fly fishing this area in previous years but only after the first of June when the salmon had changed their feed from the shrimp to young herring and needlefish. During those times, I hooked many fish using the *hunt-drift-cast* method.

Using this method, I would cruise the immense waters where fish would be surfacing, watching for surface signs like hovering gulls or concentrations of sea ducks. I would also use binoculars to search the flat water surfaces for the tell-tale roils that indicated salmon feeding. Once I had located surface feeding action, I would motor toward the activity, throttling down as I came near the fish, then turn off the motor to drift parallel to the action.

With this method, as I was getting close to the fish, I would begin false-casting to be ready to drop my fly in the melee of fish-feeding action, knowing the salmon would quickly sound once they were aware of the boat. Many times a strike would occur the moment the fly struck the water, but there would often be no action and I made many further casts, some successful, before the fish moved elsewhere. While similar to chase casting, the major difference in this method lies in the fact that casting can occur for long minutes in the immediate area of the boat before the salmon move to another location.

The strike, when it comes, is typical of these gamy sport salmon. The line simply stops! A lift of the rod tip will set the hook, then the action begins! The moment these surface fish feel the bite of the hook, they are away, running meters of fly line from the reel in a dash for freedom. Without question, this is the angler's nectar, the moment when all preparation and skill result in a fish strike! I have on the rare occasion had a blueback suddenly strike the fly with no pause and immediately dash away. This, I can assure you, is a heart-stopper! Just when you feel the cast and retrieve have been a blank, suddenly there is a fish on your line. The strike is intense and, should you be quick enough to let go with your line-stripping finger, the fish will be away, with line screaming through the guides non-stop. There is no time to check whether the line has tangled on the edge of a protruding oar, fish bucket, foot or tackle box. A slight tangle in the fly line will guarantee a lost fish! This smash-strike comes in about one in four strikes. Usually it happens on the retrieve, well after you have cleared the general area of the surfacing salmon and, quite often, it occurs just as you raise the fly up from the depth. Sound familiar? Yes, a similar striking pattern for all game fish when they feel their prey, the fly in this case, is escaping.

Back to our trip. Having found these early-season fish, my partner and I both started with number eight sink-tip lines cast from three-meter fly rods, changing as the day passed to fast-sinking lines and dry lines. Leader lengths were three to four meters, for I have found in the past that, in the clear waters of the sea, fly lines and thick leaders easily spook the salmon. Flies we had in quantity as we were both tiers, including samples of all patterns that had been successful in the past but our success ratio on this trip was to haunt us.

After an hour of cruising into feeding schools we were without a single strike. This was difficult to believe in some schools, for we witnessed salmon actually leaping over our leaders and flies. There was no question the salmon could see our flies, but the patterns—silver, pink and fluorescent green colors; Pink Eve and Silver Thorn streamer patterns—were not acceptable. These are the traditional success colors for saltwater salmon, yet they did not produce a single strike in these particular active-feeding blueback schools.

I switched to another fly, much gaudier this time and tied on a number four stainless-steel hook. This pattern had a fire-red fluorescent body, pink hackle and red tail, the Flaming Frances. After a few casts I had two strikes, with one on, but lost. Frustrating minutes passed as I continued to cast, but with no further strikes. I was still using a short-strip retrieve and often watched the bluebacks surfacing within centimeters of my fly.

Then, on one cast, I let the fly sit in the water for a moment before the retrieve and had a solid strike. The fish was a strong one of about one kilogram, who ran out several meters of the fly line and, on two occasions, took me into my backing. When he finally came near the boat, we spotted the hook embedded in his side, likely hooked there after the strike during a rolling, twisting action, which had pulled the hook out of his mouth but rehooked in his side as the pulling line unravelled around his body.

My partner, meanwhile, has also changed flies and, following my suggestion of letting the fly sit for a moment, then using a very slow retrieve, soon hooked a fish. This one rolled and cartwheeled on the surface as it fought his light six-pound leader. It gave several long runs, never quite taking line to the reel, rather, making him strip line and fight it as he played it to the boat. It was a beauty, fully one kilogram in weight and silver as the winter moon.

By this time, we had drifted past the feeding school and I started the motor to move to another feeding flurry of gulls, watching once more for the feeding, surfacing bluebacks. This time, I found a long crescent of water birds with surfacing salmon in the middle, among many concentrations of surface feed.

Cutting the motor, we drifted slowly to within casting range but, after no strikes, we wondered if our sink-tip line had gone underwater too fast and too far. We switched to our dry line outfits and, using the slow retrieve, within moments, were again into bright silver, flashy bluebacks, leaping and struggling as only coho salmon can.

These two came easily to the boat and then there was calm! Where once there had been a furious surface commotion, now only a few tardy birds still lingered. We stood, amazed at this sudden change, searching for more bird and surface activity, motoring throughout the area for an hour, stopping at any location where a bird was on or near the water, but the bite was off.

Blueback fly fishing is unique as a result of its setting, usually in the open water, far from shore, where the sheer immensity of the experience can overwhelm the angler. Often, I have tried to triangulate for a point of reference, but have found this only partially satisfying to my sense of knowing where one is, the knowledge I require to satisfy the basic need of a location. One tool that has helped me to return to the current known spot is a plastic float dropped overboard when I have a strike. With the drift of tide and wind, I have used this as a reference to return to the area where the school was holding. Another reference point can be the tide line with its distinct flotsam. This can easily become a site clue but be prepared— salmon do not always move in ways where you can use this guide. The angler will usually have a fantastic fly fishing day then return to the same general location only to find the fish have moved, forcing him to hunt once again.

The hunt-drift-cast method for open water fly fishing is usually practiced during the early season but, as you have read, it is dependent upon surface feed. A tide line, marked by small pieces of flotsam is one area that I will hunt and I have often found small schools concentrating in the middle or on the edge of this material. A concentration of gulls, particularly the small Bonaparte's gull or a mew gull, is a major sign and a leaping fish will often betray the school. Once found, care and caution must be the by-word as you approach these surfacing fish. If you are successful, it is possible that you will drift with a school for up to an hour before they finally sound.

4

Beach and Estuary Fly Fishing

Autumn Beach Fly Fishing for Coho

How well I remember pushing the beach fly fishing season for coho one weekend late in September. Trying the beaches at Black Creek, where I'd heard there were a few hook-nosed northerns showing, excited me. The weather forecast had a small craft warning with winds gusting to twenty-five miles per hour, so it was no wonder I looked askance at the whitecaps washing up on the beach when I arrived. However, not to be daunted, I stepped into my chest waders and waded into the pounding surf, rhythmically bobbing

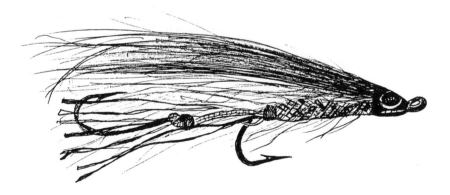

up and down to the crest of each wave as it capped just prior to reaching shore.

The rhythm was not constant though and, within minutes a wave broke over my back, sending rivulets of icy salt water down my spine and into my waders. To compound my misery on what was truly a beautiful sunny but windy autumn day, the tide change had formed concentrated masses of floating seaweed and eelgrass leaves that tangled with my fly on every second cast. However, misery does love company and I was not alone!

Down the beach, two other anglers obviously suffered the same afflictions, but continued to cast their flies. Piqued by their persistence, I continued to cast between the troughs of the incoming waves in the forlorn hope that one of the surfacing coho, which only occasionally leapt far out of casting reach, would spot my fly and strike. I was experiencing one of those unique fly fishing sport fisheries—rationalizing, as only an angler can, that casting for hours in the wet pounding surf was really the greatest!

As the rapid strip retrieve necessary for this fishery began to carve a raw groove in my right index finger—I had forgotten to bring Band-Aids—I truly began to wonder at my folly; but not for long.

A sudden jolt on the end of the fly line dispelled all those morbid considerations. There, ten meters in front of me, a bronzed hook-nosed northern coho leapt upwards, shaking the small number eight hook, caught in the side of his mouth. Two more times he tail-walked on the rolling surface but again failed to throw the hook. I lifted my rod tip high above the surf as he tore endless meters of line from the reel and watched as the fly line ended with the backing screamed through the guides and no hesitation by the fish. At least twenty meters of backing shot through the guides before the coho finally stopped his first nerve-shattering run. In the next twenty minutes, it repeated two similar runs with innumerable leaps and dogged twisting spurts. During the battle, I had waded to the shore where the bronzed, fully mature coho finally washed up on the beach with the incoming waves. This was the challenge—the thrill and I was satiated on a beautiful September day!

My first introduction to the full power of ocean coho salmon on the fly came in the late 1960s. I had come to fish for fall sea-run cutthroat trout in a stream Rod Haig-Brown had mentioned during one of our many discussions about steelhead, reinforced the previous winter when I watched Dr. Phil Power and his wife Ivy, catch and tag steelhead under the park bridge. Stories of fall harvest cutts had sent me to this beach, along with mysterious stories of wild hook-nosed northern coho caught fly fishing from the beach.

My many trips since that time, both successful and not, have been a return to flavor a truly unique fly fishing experience.

For the saltwater fly fisherman late September, October and early November provide an angling experience unmatched for excitement and trophy coho. I have met anglers who have traveled from all over to fly fish the estuary of Black Creek and other smaller coastal creeks with similar water conditions. Coho schooling near the mouth of their natal stream provide this unique fly fishery although it usually only occurs in those streams which in scientific terms, are *ephemeral* in character—they dry up during the low water summer and fall months.

These northern coho schooling in the waters at the

estuary of their home stream are the fish that will ascend the creek to spawn but, only when the waters begin to flow during the coastal southeastern gales in late October and November.

Often, beginning in mid-September, the coho will start to school offshore, constantly swimming in shallow water, testing the flow and leaching waters of their home stream, thereby give the fly fishermen the opportunity to wade in the shallows and surf to fly fish for them.

To truly appreciate the tremendous power of these fighting coho, it must be experienced first hand. They are mature adults, locally called hook-nosed northerns, weighing from three to five kilograms. Their strike varies from a slight nudge to a smash, virtually tearing the rod from the angler's hands.

Once the fish has felt the bite of the hook, he heads straight for the middle of the ocean! This first run will usually take the angler right through his fly line and well into the mandatory backing but it is often the second run that seems to continue endlessly.

Black Creek is a small stream flowing into the Strait of Georgia, on the north side of Miracle Beach Provincial Park. The estuary shallows, including the beaches in front of Miracle Beach Park and the Saratoga Beach area, are predominately cobblestone with a few large sand beaches. They are shallow beaches, almost flats, allowing the wading fly fisherman to work his fly up to distances of over a hundred meters from shore.

The foreshore from the park to the Oyster River is about two miles with much of it preserved under a park reserve status. This area, Saratoga Beach, provides excellent fly water along its full length for wading anglers. Due to a major provincial enhancement program, the sea-run cutthroat trout is relatively common in this particular area. These spunky sea-trout will readily take a fast stripped wet fly. The Oyster River is the location of the major provincial fisheries project for this species, aimed at rehabilitating that stream and lies only a few miles north of Black Creek. Numerous hatchery plantings of cutthroat trout in this watershed have made this a highly successful program.

The Black Creek estuary is but one of many estuarian areas and beaches along the coast offering the potential of this unique beach-wading saltwater fly fishing. Vancouver Island alone has over 2,000 named creeks, almost all supporting small and large runs of coho. The many thousands along the Pacific Northwest coast provide an incredible opportunity for the fly fisherman.

For beach coho fly fishing, I have found the rising tide most successful as it seems to draw the fish to the shallows, seemingly for the smell of their home stream's water but, I've often found the fish accessible on any tide. Stormy days only seem to present problems for wading, as I highlighted earlier. Many times I have cast with the wind into troughs between the waves and hooked fish in only centimeters of water.

For casting I have found a three-meter slow sink-tip fly line easiest to handle. It puts the wet fly down for the fish while, at the same time, the floating body allows for an easy pickup for the next cast. My preference is for the slow sink tip with at least a four-plus meter leader, cast from a three-meter, number eight or number nine fly rod.

Any sign of your fly line will cause these wary fish to spook. A good axiom for this type of fly fishing is

"The longer the leader the better." A long rod is helpful for longer casts to keep the fly as far from you as possible.

Fly reels are the business end for fighting these powerful fish and should hold at least 200 meters of backing. With this type of fishing always use your rod to tire the fish and fight it from the reel. If you don't take your fish to the reel quickly, flotsam will tangle your fly line, causing you to lose many fish.

Let them run—two hundred meters is a healthy distance and I have yet to have a fish strip this line beach fishing before I could gain effective control.

Many anglers now experimenting with dry lines, with and without weighted flies are having good success with either method. Success depends primarily on whether the salmon are in the shallow water, within reach of the angler's fly line.

Coho salmon school at this time of the year, located by the many jumping-jacks traveling up and down the beach. While the angler hopes every strike will bring a hook-nosed northern to the surface four out of five strikes will produce a jack coho or sea-run cutthroat trout. There can be no complaint since all these fish are a fighting fury on any fly rod battled in the ocean surf!

Watch for the cruising jack coho—these small but sexually mature males often provide the visual stimuli for the angler. Glass-calm waters seemingly devoid of salmon will suddenly erupt, with singles and schools of these jumping-jacks. They will often remain in one location forcing the angler to stalk them by walking very slowly in ultra-clear waters but, if they're moving, observe their direction of travel, parallel to the beach to determine a traveling pattern. Once discerned, wade to intercept them and be ready for action.

Seals are the primary salmon predator in these areas but they are a blessing for the fly fisherman, for their presence usually makes the salmon move closer to shore. While the smaller jumping-jacks are not the main quarry for the fly fisherman, they are often indicators of the presence of a school of large, mature coho.

Chest waders are a must for this exciting fly fishing. They allow the angler to move out in the deeper shallows and give warmth from the constant chill of the salt water. Move very slowly when fish are in the area. Possibly looking like predatory seals and sea lions, moving waders can frighten salmon.

It has been my observation that most fly anglers will release their fish, however, I recommend a small landing net to hold fish while the angler makes the long, slippery walk back to shore. Once played out, the most effective method for the larger coho is beaching—sliding the fish up on shore. I am reluctant to count the number of times I have had a good fish wrap me with line and leader, suddenly breaking off when I attempted to grasp him in the shallows, 100 meters from shore.

The most effective flies I have found are those skimpily tied on stainless steel long shank hooks. The best color patterns are those with silver, pink, purple, red, blue and lime green and I have generally found a pattern with a red or silver body the most effective.

In my earlier years, while I was first experimenting with this unique fishery, I tried numerous experimental fly patterns, using whatever materials I could find that I felt would attract these fish. An old, torn, red plastic raincoat proved a key material when cut in thin strips and used as body material, providing a translucent red body, appealing to cruising fish.

Bob Weir, my long-time fly fishing friend, tied several of these patterns, finally perfecting the current, *very effective* one, dubbed Cathy's Coat, tied with or without a red tail, polar bear streamer and pink or orange hackle.

Interestingly, popular sea-run cutthroat patterns like the Mickey Finn, the Professor and the Polar Coachman are usually very effective, particularly for the smaller jacks.

Autumn beach fly fishing for coho is a rare trophy sport sometimes providing fish weighing from one to ten kilograms. You will never know until the fish strikes! Beach fly fishing opportunities throughout the Pacific Northwest are certain to increase with the recent recognition of the critical importance of small streams for coho and the increasing number of enhancement programs on these streams!

Midsummer Estuary Fly Casting for Pinks
Pinks at Kuhushan Point

The cry, "Here they come! Here they come!" echoed up and down the cobblestone beach between Kuhushan Point and the estuary of the Oyster River. It was a cry pumping the angler's nectar, adrenaline, into the half-dozen fly fishermen lining the beach. Immediately, the false-casting began, to lengthen the fly line in preparation of that school of silver pink salmon swimming toward them, parallel along the beach, porpoising and leaping as they moved within casting range of each angler. As this leaping school passed each angler, the continual, exuberant cries of, "One on!" broke the silence. For those anglers who were not successful—usually about half of them—the casting and retrieving was intense as they sought to hook any stragglers who had either left the school or were in the general area in front of the angler.

This pattern repeated itself during the day, through the ebbing tide, into the slack and on into the flood. Anglers came and went, seemingly in unison with the traveling schools but the schools of pink salmon continued to come, moving up the beach then down, giving the anglers that long-sought-after chance at these spunky fighting salmon.

This specific fly fishery is but one example of the efforts of over 8,000 volunteers in British Columbia in a specific program on the Oyster River initiated by the Oyster River Salmon Enhancement Society, with the cooperation of federal fisheries. Pink salmon are native to the Oyster River, but numerous environmental problems, channelization of the river and clear-cut watershed logging virtually wiped out the native run of pinks. A decade ago the society constructed a rearing and spawning channel for incubating pink salmon eggs taken from the Quinsam River. In 1988, the river received its first return of 30,000 pinks. Since then, the yearly return has averaged well over 50,000 pink salmon on both odd and even year cycles, a credit to volunteer community effort and involvement.

Pink salmon are likely the most evolved of all salmon species, so much so that serious environmental damage, or a river disaster could wipe out their river-specific run. They are the only salmon race without adults for a period of time. Scientists claim the odd and even year races of pink salmon are genetically separate, a sobering thought when we consider the conservation needs of these fish.

Adult pink salmon travel from the ocean into their natal stream any time between June and September, depending on their specific genetic signals for that location. They tend to spawn in the lower reaches of their stream and the young hatch in January or February, depending on water temperature, remaining in the gravel until March or April. At this time, they wriggle up through the gravel and, almost immediately, begin to move downstream to the estuary, usually traveling at night. Once the fry have reached the salt water, they will remain in the estuary for up to a month before beginning their northern migration in the Pacific where they will spend about eighteen months before returning to spawn. Pinks appear to be less specific in their return to their natal stream, with many wandering into other watersheds.

For the fly fisher, pink salmon offer an exciting quality and quantity fishery during the late summer months as well as a special open water blueback fishery in the early spring. Sadly, federal management of this salmon ignores the sport fisher, with the result that ancient, early twentieth century *no stream fishery* regulations still apply, in one of the classic examples of insensitive salmon fisheries management.

Hopefully, federal managers will soon recognize the importance of the sport fishery and will regulate various limited entry regulations for freshwater pink salmon fishing, but in the meantime, we do have the tidal saltwater fishery and what a fishery it can be for the fly fisher!

Before the major pink enhancement programs resulting from the Salmonid Enhancement Program (SEP), most pink fisheries concerned even years, the time of the major run returns in British Columbia. Minor returns did occur in odd years, but did not result in an intense sport fishery. SEP projects have now changed this and this fishery is available every year.

At the beginning of this chapter, I spoke of the close-to-shore habits of the returning adults, making them accessible to wading fly fishers. Speculating on the cause, I feel fresh water from the fish's natal stream is the major factor. At the beaches near the rivers I have waded pinks seem to move very close to shore on all tides. At times they will remain in one specific location, quite obvious by their flashing sides, circling steadily. Jumpers are always present, providing the visual clue to the location of these schools. On these beaches, particularly where tidal movement is limited, I have often moved ever-slowly to within casting range of a spiraling school and hooked fish after fish after fish, until my arms were sore and my back stiff from all the action. It was only

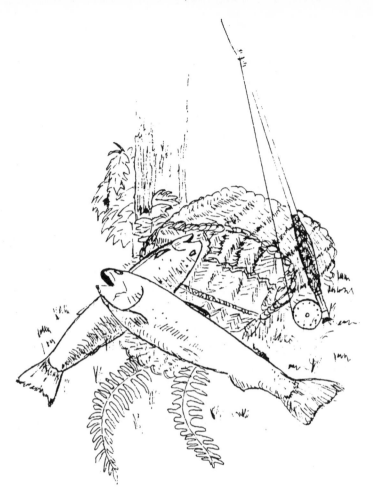

when shadows or movement from another angler or seal spooked the school that they moved off.

In these situations, I feel pockets of fresh water play a prominent role and these are what hold the school in these locations. Along the Kuhushan beaches the dominant tide moves south to north, from the Oyster River to the point, moving the fresh water from the river, close to shore where the pinks travel.

One vivid memory of pink fishing in this location involved a trip with my Okanagan fishing partners, who had traveled to my home on Vancouver Island for their annual summer salmon fishing trip. On our first trip, my outboard motor had packed it in, as the saying goes, and we were without a boat until I had a replacement motor.

Their arrival had coincided with the arrival of the pinks at Kuhushan Point. As both were fly fishers, we spent three glorious, calm, summer days hooking and releasing pinks along the cobblestone beaches. We arrived late in the afternoon on our first day to find several anglers, fly fishers and spin casters working the mouth of the river, where a school of pinks had pocketed. Space was at a premium but the fish were there! It was a calm, warm day, the kind made for light chest waders although, as each day progressed, the ocean cold soon seeped through, chilling our bodies.

Occasional leapers farther north on the sand beach gave away the location of another school of fish. As no other anglers were covering these fish, we moved toward them, wading out, trying to reach these deeper salmon. I had supplied both my friends with Pink Eve patterns although Bob, an expert fly tier, had put together several similar patterns before the trip.

Bob's first fish came almost immediately! We were chattering about the *how to* of this fishery, when a fish took softly, a prime buck just showing the beginnings of a hump and kype—the pink salmon identification giveaway. This fish took Bob well into his backing, but was soon at his side and released. Marilyn took her first fish on the sandy shallows a few minutes later. She was soon into a second, then a third, while Bob and I continued to cast in the area, waiting for our inevitable strike. The opening to this chapter occurred during this trip, as the cry of "Here they come!" punctuated the beach throughout our three glorious days. We came to several important conclusions about this fishery through our many discussions during and after this trip.

The first was obvious; be there at the right time! Each stream that spawns pink salmon has its own fish arrival calendar. The last week of July is the earliest I have yet seen pinks at Kuhushan Point but I have waded for these fish as early as July 1 on other streams. Like all fly fishers, I keep a diary and have found this vital for planning trips.

A second conclusion focused on the condition of the fish. Those caught close to the mouth of the river were often darker and showed the characteristic yellow sides of early spawning condition. Those caught farther down the beach, away from the river mouth, tended to be much cleaner, with a more pronounced silver side, some as bright as polished silver dinnerware!

Chest waders were a must, for we found that some schools would not come close to the shore, choosing to stay at a range that required water under the arms during casting. Suffice it to say though, that a few schools actually swam right at our feet, particularly if we did not move our legs. We even found it necessary to turn and cast toward shore for these fish, although this was the exception.

The most successful fly patterns were those which had silver and pink in combination, like the Pink Eve. The best hook size was a number four or six in a long shank; Mustad 34011.

Fly rods varied considerably—a heavy rod in a size eight or larger soon became tedious to cast. A number seven rod of three to four meters was the happy medium, providing a light reel was used. With this combination, we found we could fish most of the day without tiring.

Fly lines ranged from dry lines to fast sinking sink tips. My preference held with a medium sinking three-meter sink tip tied to 200 meters of backing. Bob and Marilyn preferred dry lines and we never felt it necessary to use a wet line. We always used three to five meters of six- or eight-pound leaders to ensure the fly line would not spook the fish. On occasion, I have covered a school of pinks with my fly line, to astounding reaction—the water literally boiled under the fly line as the school bolted for deep water!

For those salmon we did kill, keeping them fresh and cool was a serious problem at first. We could not leave the fish on the beach to spoil in the summer heat if they survived the seagulls so, our solution was to use a cloth or gunny sack placed in a heavy, aerated plastic carrying bag anchored with rocks in the cool ocean water. We found we had to check this often because of warm incoming tidal water or outgoing tides but this was not a task.

It was interesting that we all felt it necessary to take rest periods on the beach; one, to rest sore backs and two, to observe where other schools of pinks were congregating. It was also very difficult to get a solid grip on the baseball- to melon-sized cobblestones!

While we may have located one specific school and fished it for a time, there were always other schools with fish who had not seen our flies. When we first fished these new schools we often hooked several fish before our success was reduced.

During other trips, I occasionally found the pinks were not concentrated near the shore. Then I would take my boat and fish a mile or so from shore, where the pinks were showing on the surface, particularly near tide lines. These were concentrated schools, like those at the beach, but traveling and likely heading for other river systems. I found I could motor in front of these schools and cast a wet line to sink my fly to their depth. It was almost an imperative to have the fly in front of the school to hook fish.

My many experiences beach fishing for pinks has given me a great respect for these spunky sport salmon on a fly rod. Their dogged struggles, incredible tenacity and their uncanny ability to throw the hook is unmatched. Unfortunately, the many degrading references to these fish from the commercial sector, "those slimers," "the sheep of the sea," has left this species with a much underrated name.

It is time that the sport sector be given a fair chance to angle for these salmon in fresh water as well as salt!

5

Tackle And Equipment

Of all the chapters I have written in this book, this is the one with which I have had the most difficulty. An angler's equipment is a very personal choice and what will work for one angler will often be quickly discarded by another. Having said that, I feel we can all learn from the experiences of others and what follows is a list of recommendations I have found effective and useful for saltwater fly fishing.

Fly Rods

Saltwater salmon fly fishing rods need length and power. These two criteria should be the focus when selecting the main artillery for fly fishing. The plethora of choices available make it foolish for me to recommend one or the other company's equipment. With the rapid changes occurring annually in rod materials, design and make, it is likely that any recommendation may be outdated even before this book is published. What I can recommend are those tangible needs which many years of experience have taught me.

Rods must withstand boat-use abuse. Dealing with large fish, rods often get dropped for a variety of reasons; while the net is used, when switching from one outfit to another or when simply transporting them to and from the boat. The rods also take considerable bruising from being bounced in transit or when boat rails bang them. Naturally, you try to protect them but, on occasion, such as when chase casting, speed and haste are necessary for success. It is at these times you will be happy you have considered boat-use abuse at time of purchase. On the sides—the gunnels—of my boat, I have sets of neoprene rod holders attached to the rails, many more than I need but placed in locations where I can immediately place my rods when I move the boat.

Reels

Once, while showing my outfits to an interested fly fisherman, he remarked how fly fishing for salmon must cost a fortune but when I told him how many years it had taken me to obtain the specific outfits I was showing him, he withdrew his previous statement, adding "it certainly is cheaper than a season's ski pass or a golf club membership."

Without question, the most expensive items in my fly fishing equipment are the reels, the business end of salmon fly fishing and, unlike trout fishing, where the majority of the fish can be played by hand using the reel simply as a pickup spool for your fly line, salmon *must* be played from the reel. They are simply too large and the ocean is too big to contain them with hand stripped fighting.

Again, as with fly rods, a glut of choices are available on the market so I use a simple set of rules for my reels: they must be salt-corrosive resistant, carry 200 meters of backing and 100 meters of running line, as well as my fly line, be as light as possible and have a guaranteed drag system that will never cinch up during a long fish run.

With these expectations, one can realize there will be a healthy price for each reel. Yes, *each* reel! While the beginner can start with a single reel and have considerable success, eventually a minimum of three reels will be required—one for each of the three outfits you should have ready on your boat.

I have mentioned many times that, on each trip I take for a day's open water salmon fly fishing, I have several fly casting outfits set up and ready to fish. I cannot emphasize more strongly how important it is to be prepared! These outfits are classified based on the three depths I anticipate fishing:

Surface Casting Outfit

If there is one fly line that could be called the all-purpose line for saltwater salmon fly fishing it would be the sink tip. In its variations; three-, six- and ten-meter, slow, medium and fast sinking tips, it covers most situations facing the saltwater salmon fly fisherman.

This all-purpose outfit is a three- or six-meter fast

sink tip. The floating portion of the line allows me to lift the fly line quickly for another cast if necessary, while the sink-tip head places the fly below the surface in areas that best imitate crippled bait fish.

This all-purpose surface casting outfit is the one I place in the top rungs of my rod holders for instant action. Often, when I start from the launch, I will do several false-casts, preparing a length of fly line for instant casting. After hooking the fly to the hook holder near the rod handle, I will strip in the loose fly line in a clear area on the bottom of the boat beside me or in an empty fish bucket, where it will not hook up when I need to make quick casts. This is the one time I make certain that the leader is shorter than the distance from hook holder to the tip of the rod. I can assure you there is nothing more frustrating than being in the flurry of action and not being able to get the fly line sliding through the tip of the rod. This is my one concession to a short leader length while fishing in the clear waters of the ocean. If I am packing a fair amount of gear on the floor of the boat that particular day I will use the fish bucket as a stripping basket to hold the loose line while I travel.

Anchored Deep Wet Line Outfit

My second outfit is the deep line, which I use from an anchored position. This is the outfit I use the majority of the time and have found that, during the past three seasons, I have gone through an average of two complete outfits each year. The business end of this outfit is the shooting head, which I attach to a thirty-meter fast sinking running line, using the loop system, attached to 100 meters or more of reel backing. The most effective shooting head appears to be a number eleven weight. I do have complete sets, a number eight, nine, ten and eleven, a 750 grain, and a heavier saltwater express head and will often change to these different weights in different water or tide conditions but, as ten meters is my favored anchored fly fishing depth, I find the number eleven head the most effective and enjoyable to use.

Surface Dry Line Outfit

My third outfit is a dry line used for covering fish-surfacing *windows,* for fast, surface, racing bait fish imitation or occasionally, for herring ball action. Many saltwater fly lines are now available and I would recommend these to you. Make certain to match the line to the rod and use the rule of add one number for saltwater use; for example, use a number nine line with a number eight rod. Using this system, I find I have an increase in distance, giving me additional retrieve time on my flies.

Tournament Floats

These small brightly colored buoys are an invaluable asset on open salt water. I always carry sets with me on my boat and keep them readily available. We have all heard the jokes of marking an X on the water (or your boat) to show the location of the fish—well, this is how you do it! These buoys have a weight attached to 100 or more meters of line that, when thrown overboard, anchors the buoy at the location selected.

For the fly fisherman, they are extremely useful to mark a drop-off location where you would like to anchor, to box a particular area of open water where salmon may be located or to mark the edge of a school of herring for casting purposes.

Stripping Basket

This tool can be very effective in several ways. On your boat, it will provide a safe storage if you have difficulty clearing an area at your feet when you strip your fly line. It does not have to be worn around your waist in the traditional manner, but can be placed at your feet. I find a plastic fish tub an excellent substitute.

For beach wading, a stripping basket can be most effective where there is a large concentration of flotsam seaweed drifting on the surface. Eel grass is particularly frustrating, as it will continually tangle with your drifting stripped fly line, as will the floating masses of sea lettuce.

Binoculars

I have often found my binoculars have meant the difference between success and near-failure on many trips. Bird activity, particularly gulls, is often the secret to finding salmon. As one partner emphatically exclaimed one day, "Birds don't lie!" When fishing, I will constantly scan the horizon with my binoculars, looking for bird activity. If it persists, it is like a magnet I can't resist!

Charts

There are few items as valuable to the saltwater angler as marine charts. These are your maps of the undersea world, providing an incredible encyclopedia of information. I spend hours annually, pouring over the charts in the areas I fish, looking for those specific drop-offs, shoals and deep holes that tend to hold salmon. Make certain you have a complete set for all areas you fly fish. It is remarkable the information they provide—especially the deep holes and drop-off areas where salmon concentrate.

Tide Guides

Like marine charts, tide guides are an absolute must for the fly angler. Each coastal community produces a very useful yearly guide but, to be certain, at

110

the beginning of each calendar year purchase the *Tide and Current Tables* for the areas you plan to fish.

Fly Boxes

These must not be metal, which guarantees rust and must be avoided at all costs if you are to protect your flies. I would hate to count the number of flies I have lost because I did not follow this rule.

When fishing from a boat, where you do not have to carry a fishing vest with numerous pockets, a large fly box is useful. I find the new plastic *pistol cases* particularly effective for my flies and for boat use. The neoprene holds flies well and they do not fall out when bounced about in the boat. The larger space also allows for a large selection for display of effective patterns and sizes within those patterns. I keep two kits ready—the second with weighted flies that I find necessary in many saltwater conditions.

Scissors

This is one tool I use repeatedly during a day's fishing. It sits on the dash, where it is easily accessible. Knives and nail clippers are useful but usually, only for cutting line. Scissors, on the other hand, can trim flies and precisely trim knots.

Needle-nose Pliers

This is another tool that has a prominent place on my dashboard, used primarily to release fish, including dogfish and rockfish. Yes, dogfish and rockfish are active strikers and exciting fighters on your salmon fly when fished either too slow or too near the bottom.

Net

An amazing variety of nets are available on the market but, beware—those made with some materials are real hook-grabbers! I rarely use a net unless I plan to keep a fish. I feel the salmon's body weight, when lifted, does serious damage to some internal organs. I will also never lift a salmon by his gills and, certainly, never use the *bass mouth lift* we see so often on television shows. One effective tip is to mark the regulation lengths of the various salmon species on the gunnel of your boat with a waterproof marker. If I am considering keeping a fish, I have found most salmon fairly passive when I lift them in my net and place them on the gunnel for measuring.

Depth Sounder

I cannot emphasize how valuable a tool the modern depth sounder is. I would recommend a middle-of-the-line unit with a good depth readout. Used with your charts, the depth sounder will help locate steep and deep drop-off locations and underwater peaks. It will also help find the underwater kelp beds and compact masses of bait fish.

Hook Sharpener

Do I need to say anything? I have a habit of sharpening and de-barbing my hooks at home however, in all my kits, I carry some version of a hook sharpener for regular use. Hooks must be tacky sharp, so use your thumbnail, poking it slightly with the hook, as the guide.

First Aid Kit with *Many* Band-Aids

Salt water is extremely abrasive. I find I regularly use Band-Aids to cover my right index finger, the one on which I constantly strip my fly line. I find it does not affect my reflex action on a strike and, with its protection, ensures a pleasurable day fly fishing on salt water. Always carry a standard first aid kit and carefully check personal prescriptions regularly.

Fish Chest

Your boat should include a fish chest of some type to hold ice for those salmon you put in the creel. For beach fishing, a wet gunny-sack provides the best portable protection.

Float to Anchor Rope for Quick Release

Attach a small bumper float to your anchor rope with a quick-snap release so you can chase large running salmon if it becomes necessary.

Beach Waders

I use two sets of waders for most of my beach fishing, making the choice when I reach the beach area based on the temperature that day. The ocean water temperature is constant and either a pair of neoprene waders or a boot-insulated thin-shelled wader is acceptable during the summer and fall months for chasing salmon. Coastal weather is very changeable and you will likely spend considerable time standing in one location with ocean water above your hips, so body warmth is very important. If I were to apply one rule to which waders to wear, I would consider how long I will be fishing, then select body warmth if I am expecting to spend more than two hours in the water.

Equipment is personal and these are but a few of the many personal items that have brought me success saltwater fly fishing. Considering my boat, with its many attachments or my fly kits of materials, reminds me that what I have found constant one year changes the next, as weather patterns change, kelp beds come and go and salmon movement patterns vary. Many new items reach the retail market annually and I am quick to try these to improve the opportunities I will have or to give me a keener edge. I find that I discard many items after each season, either because they are too clumsy or they simply don't work but this constant search and experimentation is all part of the sport of open saltwater salmon fly fishing.

6

Saltwater Flies

Introduction

When I began experimenting with saltwater salmon fly fishing, I tried the many bucktails known as effective salmon flies but I quickly learned there was a difference. I became obsessed with the Cowichan Bucktail, because of its extra thick polar bear hair body, thinking that, by its sheer size, it would attract salmon. Not so and, in fact, this particular obsession almost became my saltwater salmon fly fishing nemesis!

In those earlier days, while experimenting with this fly, (try casting a thick polar bear hair bucktail) I soon began to tie skimpier and skimpier patterns be-

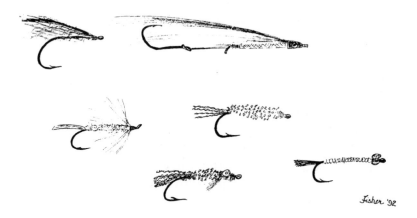

cause of the sheer weight and clumsiness of a true bucktail. If you have never done so, try fly casting these true bucktails tied on a number 3/0 or 4/0 hook with a number one trailer hook. It is a challenge, even to the most skilled fly fisherman.

While experimenting, I felt the length of the fly was important and, to preserve this, I would use a pair of pliers to cut off the main hook at the bend. This lightened the fly considerably and proved moderately effective for casting but, as I tied skimpier and skimpier patterns, rather than cut the main hook, I simply eliminated the trailer hook. All this occurred at the time I realized that a slow retrieve was far more effective in hooking salmon. As a result, I began tying with smaller hooks: number 2/0, 1/0, 1, 2 and even number 4, ending in very sparse streamer patterns. The sheer simplicity of the patterns I now use astounds most conventional fly fishermen, but they work!

In analyzing my many successful patterns, I have come to a simplistic, but quantum leap, concept for saltwater salmon fly fishing—bait fish do not have hackles! Rather, silver streamer simplicity appears to succeed for saltwater salmon fly fishing.

For many years, I have watched coho fry in an aquarium, curious to see if observation of behavior patterns would help in my fishing. I was particularly interested in territorialism and often watched the most dominant fry hold a particular position in the aquarium by what can best be called a *body threat posture.* If another fry intruded in the area of the dominant fry, the latter would dart out to the edge of what he considered his territory and, by posturing, including a raised dorsal fin and open mouth, he would turn the intruder away. This is the only time I have seen an extended appendage in coho and then only in the dominant fry. The intruder would have noticeable lower fins, often sleek to the body. It has also been my experience that bait fish in panic flight also keep their fins close to their body—a true, sleek, streamer fly position. For this reason, I now feel a protruding hackle is a no-no for most salmon flies.

As always there is one exception—exposed gills, particularly when a young salmon or bait fish is tired, usually following a panic survival dash, tells me that a streak of pink or red, isolated on the underside of the head of a fly will add one more element to entice a strike. This, I have found to be true with salmon and I now often use short and skimpy red or pink material tied on the throat of my flies to imitate this visual stimulus.

As my flies became skimpier and skimpier, I soon found myself using nothing but polar bear hair tied to a silver stainless steel hook and these produced effective flies in many locations. Variations in color—pink, red and green, produced successful flies, which I subsequently named Butler's White, Butler's Red & White, Butler's Pink and the Green Herring. The former names were given for the highly-productive salmon fly fishing location immediately south of Quadra Island in the Strait of Georgia, where a great deal of my salmon saltwater fly fishing experimentation occurred.

Hook size appears to be significant for salmon strikes, particularly when fishing young bait fish. In my fly box, I have tied sets of successful patterns on hook sizes number six through number 5/0. Matching hook size to the bait appears to produce more strikes, although I believe in the magnum theory—the fatal attraction of the biggest. This works with many fish and wildlife species, duck decoys being the most obvious. With fish, we do know that bigger is better, providing it does imitate some natural food source. Steelheaders, for example, take clear advantage of this natural phenomenon with the vast variety and sizes of imitation egg lures used.

One of the more visually exciting experiences rewarding the salmon fly fisherman is the element of competition in a feeding school of salmon. Like the tip of an iceberg, only a small sample of the feeding activity is visible from the surface but, underneath, on those rare occasions when clear water and light refraction permit, the fly fisherman is treated to a fascinating world of prey and predator, individual and group action.

On several occasions I have watched what, I felt, was the element of competition play a major role in strikes at my fly. In each situation, I was casting to the edge of a herring school. It was the obvious nervousness of the herring, their repeated, sudden, darting back to the safety of kelp fronds that told me there were feeding salmon in the vicinity. On one occasion, I could see through the water at least eight meters when I became aware the herring had parted, leaving my fly exposed, between two sections of the bait school. Coho suddenly appeared near my fly—sudden is the only word, for at one moment the water was clear and empty and the next, there were finning coho staring at my fly. One darted at the fly, swerving at the last moment to circle again while, at that same instant, a second darted in and snapped up the fly. It is an image I will carry forever!

On another occasion, while beach fishing for pink salmon the water clarity and light refraction gave me the opportunity to watch the action of a school of fifty or more salmon when I presented my fly. At this time,

I was standing on a sand bar, allowing me to watch the salmon in a depression about fifty meters in front and below me. When I cast, I was careful my fly line did not cover the school, for this, I have learned, is certain to spook these fish in shallow beach areas. In this situation, I first cast my Pink Eve fly to the side of the school, then began a slow retrieve, watching for a fish to dart out to strike the fly. As the fly came past the school, several fish began to slowly follow. Like a growing arm from an amoeba, I watched the slow flowing of the dark shadow of the school, now following the leaders, following my fly. I was entranced at the sheer poetry of motion of these fish and the often-repeated term, "sheep of the sea," used by commercial salmon fishermen when they talk about pink salmon, came to mind. During the first cast no fish struck, although the leaders followed the fly for a good three meters. On the third cast, which produced the same result as the first, a fish suddenly darted forward and took the fly.

The competition in this flowing school likely lead to the strike from that first fish. Certainly, it contributed equally to the next series of strikes and hooked fish, eventually leaving my arms sore and weak after playing so many of these powerful salmon.

Be warned that rust on your flies is inevitable! During my first few years of active saltwater fly fishing I was appalled at the end of a day's fishing and, particularly at the end of the season, to find the majority of my flies beyond saving simply because of rust—I mean rust *throughout!* Precious body material, like polar bear hair, was stained in varying ranges of yellow-brown and hooks dropped pieces of rust-brown material, staining the fly boxes and other hooks in the boxes. It took a while, but I eventually replaced all flies in this sad state with stainless steel. Today, all my patterns are tied with stainless steel or salt-resistant hooks, but even this can be insufficient. Materials like tinsel and silver threads will, in time, become oxidized and stain flies.

Some of the successful ways I have found of combating rust include the following; Always be certain your flies are dry before placing them in fly boxes. To do this, I will never place a fly in the box until I am home. On the water, I carry a small cigar box on the dashboard of my boat, where all flies are placed after use. The wood in the box acts as a moisture absorber, effectively drying the flies during boat traveling time.

Rather than having a series of small fly boxes, which are most confusing when selecting particular patterns, I use one of the new plastic pistol carrying cases to store them. These come in several sizes, are inexpensive and hold flies amazingly well. This kit gives me freedom of selection without confusion and travels well in the boat.

When I tie flies with silver tinsel thread—the most common thread I use for my salmon patterns—I use liberal amounts of head cement, often applying two or more applications, to ensure a watertight seal against salt water.

I recommend that you wash your flies in fresh water when you come home. While often a tedious chore, it can be done at the same time the reels are washed. I have found that, unless flies are carefully dried after rinsing, rust staining will still occur.

The revolution in fly-tying materials during the past decade, along with my insatiable desire to experiment with new materials, to create that super fly, has led me to create a basic pattern with which I now tie the vast majority of my salmon patterns. As one of my partners once referred to it, "Barry, it's just another of your plain Jane patterns but boy, does it work!" Work it has, as this one experience will reveal:

A late July evening telephone call from the western editor of a fly fishing magazine was, on that rare occasion, a chance call preceding a day of that old angling adage, "You should have been here yesterday!"

That summer day, I had hunted for salmon in the waters surrounding Hornby Island, one of the northern Gulf islands of the Strait of Georgia. I had located a school of stationary young herring off Nash Bank reef, marked by the green spar at Tribune Bay. It had been midday when I reached the spar, about an hour prior to the low tide slack at 12:30. During the last part of the ebb tide, I anchored about fifteen meters, a good casting distance from the kelp on the reef. A large school of young herring were seeking safety from feeding salmon in the now low water, protruding shoal and kelp, but many were stranded outside the safety of the kelp by the sheer numbers of those who had found refuge there. Leaping coho grilse were continually plopping on the surface at the edge of the herring school and, occasionally a mature two-plus kilogram coho surfaced.

I was experimenting with the new fly, tied with silver thread and using silver tinsel chenille for a body. It was a simple pattern, something I have found in the past is usually the most effective for salmon and yet, used basic materials which would, hopefully, entice those exciting saltwater fish. It was tied on a 1/0 Mustad O'Shaughnessy number 34007 sea hook and I used a range of lead wire body weights to take the fly down below the herring.

As I was setting up in the front of the boat, a

shower of herring surfaced beside the kelp and a large splash indicated a good-sized coho had torn through the bait school. I began casting to that area, letting the fly sink below the school of bait fish, testing the flow of the tidal current. A few casts later, when I felt I had the proper flow, I mended the line following my cast into the tide flow, similar to the mend I use when casting upstream in a river.

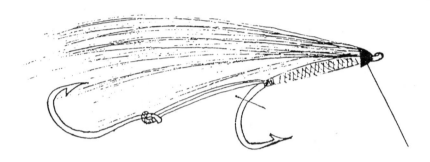

Mending is the process of rolling or flipping extra fly line upstream to give the fly time to drift naturally before the current catches the line and causes the fly to streak across the river. Mending fly line is a specific skill I have found extremely valuable in saltwater fly fishing when faced with tidal surface currents and I want to get my fly down to the fish. This time, when I had mended the line, I began a slow but steady short strip retrieve, mesmerized by the sight of the thousands of young herring above the fly line.

The line stopped—no jerk, no smash strike, just a halt, as if I had hooked a snag. I lifted the rod and, suddenly, the herring school parted, to reveal a twisting coho at the end of the fly line. It had been a very soft strike, but there was no doubt it was a good salmon. The fish shot under the herring, under the boat and headed for the deeper water. I managed to swing the rod around the front of the boat, picked up the slack line by stripping it through my fingers and then, watched all the loose line at the bottom of the boat rapidly disappear as the fish brought me to the reel.

The coho fought as only these bright silver salmon can—surface leaping, thrashing and dogged runs in wide arcs around the boat. When he finally came to the net, he was thoroughly exhausted and I couldn't wait to get my fly out again for the next fish. In the next two hours, I netted three coho and hooked and lost three others. Unfortunately, I had a late afternoon meeting so I finally pulled up the anchor and headed home, vowing to be on the water at that location, much earlier the next day.

That was the evening David called. I invited him to experience this outstanding fishery and he agreed so we made arrangements to meet in the morning. I planned to be at the reef an hour into the ebb, when the action had been the greatest and it was a fortunate choice!

I was waiting with my boat at 8:00 A.M. at the boat ramp when David arrived in his station wagon. We exchanged introductions, then launched the boat. I had warned David that Vancouver Island mountain summer storms might cause winds on the water and they did. A fifteen-knot westerly (Qualicum) wind, gusting to twenty-five knots, made a fair chop on the water, with occasional whitecaps. This changed to a southeast wind after the tide change and resulted in the loss of two anchors, the rope sawn off each time by the weight and motion of the boat as the anchors (cement blocks) tried to hold in the compressed sandstone pockets off the reef, but it was to be our day! The herring schools were still around the kelp on the reef and the feeding salmon I had experienced the previous day were still there!

The boat run from Fanny Bay to Tribune Bay took about twenty-five minutes. While traveling, I gave David a brief history of open saltwater fly fishing for Pacific salmon. While beach, estuary and stream fishing has been relatively common for at least the past century, it has only been in recent times, with the introduction of powerful sport boats and modified fly lines, that any open water experimentation has really occurred. David had read my chapter on saltwater fly fishing in the *British Columbia Federation of Fly Fishers* book, *The Gilly,* and declared this would be a new experience for him. He had fished for salmon in Alaska's rivers, but had never cast for salmon in open salt water, as one does for feeding trout in a lake.

I told him that anglers were now seriously pursuing this sport and applying many of their feeding trout skills to salmon fly fishing. The migrating feature of salmon added a new dimension to this specific fly fishing pursuit but the skills the angler employed were essentially the same. The fly used has to imitate a feed source; the feed has to be nearby; the line has to put the fly in the location of a feeding fish; the migrating salmon have to be there and the angler has to spend the time needed to accomplish the above. All were there during our day and, aside from windblown flies and wind knots in our running lines, success was imminent!

Arriving at the spar, we discovered five boats trolling live herring in the general area of the reef. I cruised in slowly until I spotted the kelp bed, then the large school of bait herring. A few coho grilse were leaping in the area and David and I both exclaimed as a large, leaping coho, seemingly flagged the very area I wanted to drop the anchor.

In a few minutes, after dropping the anchor, clearing the bottom area of snags and preparing our tackle, I explained the technique used on the cast and retrieve. We were now using the proven Silver Thorn pattern and with a particularly obnoxious wind, it took several casts to get our lines out and ready for fishing. I was pleased with this start, soon recognizing my new partner as an experienced fly fisherman. Even with the adverse conditions of a rocking boat and a stiff wind, he was able to present the fly so effectively, it was only a matter of time before a salmon took it.

My first strike came within the first few casts. It was a bright, twisting coho, similar to yesterday's but he was on—then off! Bringing in the line, I checked the hook, retied the knot which had become askew and cast again. With this next cast, I became aware of a tremendous splash and roil in the water, in the middle of the bait herring, near the kelp.

There was no mistaking this sound! A heavy chinook salmon was obviously feeding in this school of bait. David had a strike by then and played a small grilse coho of about half a kilogram, which he released. My next strike was again the soft stop-take to which I had now become accustomed. I lifted the rod tip, but this time there was no subsequent underwater twisting flash. Instead, I felt the solid pull of a large fish. I lifted the tip, trying at the same time to clear the running line at my feet, for I knew when this fish decided to run, the line would stream from the box floor I was standing on and upon which I was stripping my line. Too late! I felt the heavy head-shake of the chinook, then watched in frustration as a wind knot blew into the streaming running line. The knotted line clicked through the first set of guides, squeezed through the third to last guide, but halted at the second to last guide. I frantically pulled on the fish, the worst thing I could have done, in retrospect, for with the pulling resistance he became more determined and the leader popped! Earlier in the summer, I had a similar experience and managed to clear the line to boat a six-kilogram chinook, but not this time!

Fate is marvelous at times. I tied on a new Silver Thorn fly, grumbling all the time, made a few false-casts and sent out my line. This time, as soon as it hit the water, a bright coho snapped it up. It was a gallant fight, compensation for the lost spring and I soon had him in the net.

This was the beginning of our day and the strikes continued throughout. Feeding fish were evident all day, through the ebb tide, at the slack and into the flood. We boated many bright coho all in the three-plus kilogram class, along with numerous grilse and jack springs. It was truly a day to remember, but success was a direct result of the basic silver-bodied fly, the Silver Thorn.

Since that particular trip, many additional trips have given me the opportunity to add to and modify this simple pattern but interestingly, when the strikes are slow, I have found I will return to that simple first pattern, knowing that new patterns with additions of color and material are not often selected by timid salmon.

A Selection of Successful Salmon Patterns

Every year, successful fly fishermen create an incredible number of new fly patterns but only a few become standards in the fly fishing literature. I have included in this chapter only those patterns I consider the elite, the tried and the proven.

Hooks vary considerably, but my preference lies with the Mustad O'Shaughnessy stainless steel hooks, numbers 34007 or 34011. The latter is a long-shank hook particularly effective in sizes number two and number four for pink salmon. However, with both numbers I tie my patterns using sizes number six through number 5/0.

The size of the hook should vary with the time of year. Obviously, in the spring when the salmon are smaller, I will use a smaller size hook, increasing this through the summer as I try to match the size of the growing herring. For most salmon fishing situations I prefer a size number one.

The clarity of salt water demands that the fly imitate some bait source such as shrimp, euphasiids, herring, needlefish or other bait fish, if salmon are to take interest and strike. For this reason, I pay particular attention to my tying threads, concentrating on silver and pink as the basic colors.

Butler's Red, White, Pink, and Green
Body: silver stainless steel hook, all sizes
Thread: silver
Wing: polar bear hair; white, green, red or pink
Comments: I have found this a highly effective fly for shallow waters.

127

Variations: Stack all three colors; vary thread for additional color.

Silver Thorn
Thread: silver
Hook: mustad 34007 or 34011; size 4 through 5/0
Tail: silver mylar tubing unraveled, or silver Krystal Flash
Body: silver metallic chenille
Head: silver thread with peacock herl
Comments: The secret to success with this fly is silver simplicity. Tie a quantity of these flies using various weights to assist with depth.
Variations: Do not change the body, but vary tail color; use polar bear hair, white and pink tails; create a peacock herl head, add silver bead chain or glass bead eyes; use a red throat.

Pink Eve
Thread: pink
Body: silver oval tinsel
Tail: fluorescent pink fishair
Wing: fluorescent pink fishair
Comments: This is the most effective and consistent fly I have found for pink salmon. It is also effective for bluebacks while open water surface fly fishing during the spring. The tinsel's ribbing appears to be critical, as does the use of pink tying thread.
Variations: Try diamond braid silver tinsel; use red and pink glass beads for optic variations; try no wing or no tail.

Pink and Red Glennis

Body: silver tinsel
Thread: silver
Wing: layered pink or red feather on top, yellow feather under
Comments: I have a particular affinity for this fly as it has hooked numerous pinks and coho for me in salt water. This fly gave me my first sense of confidence saltwater salmon fly fishing.
Variations: Use mylar tinsel tubing for body.

Cathy's Coat

Body: clear fluorescent red plastic tied in strips
Throat: brown hackle
Wing: stacked white polar bear hair
Comments: This is my Black Creek beach special. It is highly effective for fall coho at the estuary of small creeks. The tying pattern was perfected by Bob Weir.

Pink, Red, and Blue Minnow

Body: silver mylar tubing
Wing: pink feather, covered by gray mallard feather, tied down at shank
Head: painted white eye
Comments: This long-standing pattern proves itself every year. Initially, it was tied for estuary fishing, but is effective in open water, casting for coho and chinook.
Variations: Use red, blue, or green feather on wing.

129

Mrs. Nelson's Bucktail

Hook: tandem hooks with barb and shank cut off front hook

Wing: white polar bear hair with light purple stacked above—a strip of red polar bear hair of about six strands runs from the head to the shank of the trailer hook

Comments: Bill Nelson, a top Campbell River sport fishing guide perfected this pattern and a particular bucktailing method—skip fly bucktailing for coho and chinook. Bill liked to fish the shallows with this fly, often trolling in waters of a meter or less.

Art's Pink Bucktail

Hook: tandem hooks with barb and shank cut off front hook

Body: mylar tubing tied down at shank with red thread

Wing: pink polar bear hair stacked on white polar bear hair

Head: black thread with yellow eye and red pupil

Comments: Art Limber's flies are legendary! Art is a commercial fly tier who has perfected many saltwater salmon fly patterns in single hook and tandem bucktail patterns. His bucktails come in a variety of colors and makes and are a good place to start for the novice saltwater salmon fly fisher.

Pink Shrimp

Thread: pink

Body: pink fluorescent chenille, pink hackle, palmer tied

Wing: pink bucktail, tied at shank to make a case over the body and extending as a tail past the shank

Comments: Every saltwater fly fisherman will eventually tie his own variation of a pink shrimp! The importance of this pattern is the use of pink materials matching a major food source of feeding salmon.

Comet

Tail: orange bucktail, fishair

Body: oval silver tinsel

Hackle: orange

Comments: The optic variation of the Comet has always been a special favorite of mine. It has accounted for many salmon and I can count on it to work in circumstances where other flies are not successful.

Variations: Add bead chain eyes; eliminate hackle; use gold tinsel.

Fall Favorite

Body: silver tinsel

Hackle: red tied as a throat

Wing: orange bucktail

Comments: Another favorite, no pun intended. This is an effective starter fly for pinks at river estuaries.

Variations: Tail, orange or white; wing, orange and white bucktail.

Flaming Frances

Tail: red turkey feather

Body: red Angora wool

131

Hackle: red
Comments: This is my one concession to my emphasis
          that "herring do not wear hackles." It is par-
          ticularly effective when left to sit on the
          surface for a moment in an area of feeding
          bluebacks. A possible dry fly for salmon.
Variations: Use silver thread to tie.

Coronation

Tail: silver mylar tinsel unraveled
Body: silver mylar tinsel
Wing: three layers of bucktail, blue, red and white
Comments: Patterned after the much-larger bucktail.
Variations: Silver tinsel body and tail. Fishair wing.

Mickey Fin

Body: silver tinsel
Rib: oval silver tinsel
Wing: three layers of bucktail, yellow, red and yel-
          low
Comments: A traditional pattern that continues to be
          very effective.
Variations: Try red, yellow, black, or silver thread.

Silver Blue Jay

Body: silver tinsel
Wing: bright blue or robin blue polar bear hair
Comments: This pattern is particularly effective for
          coho and chinook in estuaries and rivers. On
          many occasions, while fly fishing rivers in
          October, I have hooked two, three, and even
          four different salmon species using the same
          fly. It follows the basic instruction for the
          Pink Eve, except that a rich blue color is

used. The blue color is important and should lie in the color range between navy and robin's egg blue.

Variations: Blue tail; blue fishair wing; silver bead chain optic.

7

An Alphabetical Creel of Tips

During the past decade, I have had many opportunities to concentrate on salmon fly fishing—not bucktailing but true *fly fishing*—by casting a fly on a traditional fly line. In all my time on the water, I have found it is rare to have two consecutive days when the conditions are the same. Tide changes, wind and weather variations, and salmon migration and feeding

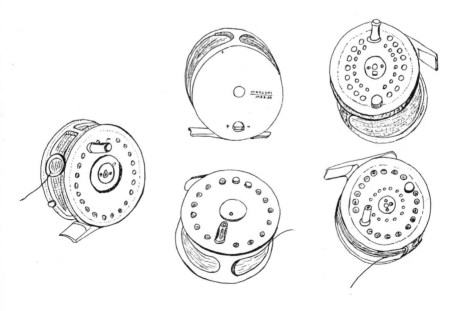

have varied in such a magnitude that I now greet each trip expecting change and I am never disappointed.

My first experiences with saltwater fly fishing over a quarter of a century ago, casting from beaches for coho and pink salmon, taught me Pacific salmon are powerful trophy fish on a fly rod. I noted then that they rarely *strike* a fly, rather they *take* it, almost as if it were a delicate morsel. But once hooked, they are an explosion of power, more often than not taking all fly line and well into the backing I have found absolutely necessary to place on my reel. The vast, open, salt water gives the fish unlimited space and I soon found they are experts at using it, sometimes it seems *all* of it!

The following alphabetized tips are the result of many fly fishing trips, both casting from the beach and from a boat. Like all tips, they come from much experimentation and many rewarding beached or boated fish. In sharing them, I hope they will save many hours of frustration and build a confidence level for the novice and experienced fly fisher, ensuring continual pleasure and success with this outstanding sport fishery. Writing to a friend recently, I lamented on the lack of fly fishermen pursuing this sport. It is a sport fishery open to the fly fishing pioneer. Likely, in the Northwest, it is the last frontier for those fish species with a sport classification. Boats, motors, fly lines and fly rods are now capable of challenging this fishery and I recommend it to you.

Anchor Location

It took many experiences and observations to realize that the most effective location from which to retrieve my fly was at the edge of a herring school. On some occasions, this has meant anchoring at the edge of a kelp bed while, on others, it has meant anchoring sixty to fifty meters from the kelp, depending on how the herring were behaving.

One daily proven tip has been the need to continually weigh anchor and move the boat, to effectively cover a moving school of bait fish. The continual harassment of the preying salmon moves the bait fish along the reef and around the bed of kelp. This movement appears to be hastened in the late flood tide when more water covers the kelp. Other boats, continually trolling or moving over the herring, also spook these bait fish, forcing them to move along the kelp. I have also observed that the white flash from a boat bottom rocking in the waves startles the bait fish, forcing them to move to another location.

Backing on Your Reel

Make certain the backing is tied to the fly line in a way that allows it to slide smoothly through the rod guides. It has been my experience that most salmon will take you past your fly line and well into your backing. On many strong fighting fish, this will happen several times, with the connecting knot sliding back and forth through the guides. Wrapping this connection with tying thread, then sealing it with head cement is an effective method to stop wear in this sensitive area.

Bait Fish

Volumes could be written about fishing around bait fish. Herring are the predominant coho and chinook feed during June and July, with sand lance or needlefish coming a close second, usually easily located near kelp, beach areas or on reefs. The fly fisher should anchor where patches concentrate, only moving his boat if the bait fish move. Feeding salmon prod at the edge of these bait fish schools and often move just under or to the side. I have found it most effective to fish under a bait fish school or on its edge, where the fly becomes exposed when they dart away for safety. In clear water, watching a salmon move in and take your fly is a sight to behold! Don't strike too soon—feel the strike before you lean back on your rod to hit the fish!

Bait Fish Schools

When the bait fish schools move, watch where the small coho (Bonaparte's and mews) gulls hover and dive. This activity, almost a symbiotic relationship between gulls and coho, indicates surfacing herring, usually forced there by feeding coho, but not all surface bait fish schools have salmon preying upon them. I have found it necessary to move from one bait fish school to another until I locate the one the fish are preying on.

Bow to The Fish

Salmon are large, lunker-sized trophy fish. When they decide to leap, their sheer power puts incredible strain on your leader. Make a habit to bow to every jump and be prepared for those unexpected leaps. I recommend you point your rod at the fish and drop the tip almost to the surface when they reach for the sky.

Bucktailing to Find Salmon

Bucktailing signifies a method of fishing not only effective for salmon, but also for larger trout in lakes. In this method, the angler trolls his fly behind the boat at varying speeds, fast enough to hold the fly just under the surface.

The origin of the term refers to the long hairs on the end of a buck deer's tail, the original material for the fly. Today, an abundance of artificial materials have acted as a successful substitute for the white and various-dyed bucktails, although deer hair is still used.

It appears the earliest reference to bucktail flies in British Columbia comes in the early part of this century, using cast salmon flies made with deer hair. These flies, called Salmon Bucktails, were tied on large hooks, usually number two or greater, with a silver tinsel body and long streamer strands of deer hair in brown, black and white from a blacktail deer's tail.

They were effective flies, according to A. Bryan Williams, British Columbia's first game warden. In his writings, he refers to the most common salmon fly fishing method as anchoring in the estuary of coastal streams and casting these various Salmon Bucktails for cohoes. According to Mr. Williams, writing in 1935 in his book, *Fish & Game In British Columbia,* "The Cohoe is an excellent sporting fish, he will take the fly well both in the sea and fresh water whenever conditions are favorable ... he (the coho) jumps much more frequently and dashes about in such a wild way that considerable skill is required to play him."

Bucktailing is a salmon fishing method initiated and perfected in the Strait of Georgia. This particular method of salmon fishing appears to come from the Cowichan Bay area, where bucktail flies were trolled from the rowboats in the area. With the introduction of outboard motors, bucktailing flourished. Today, large, full bucktails with trailer hooks are commonly called Cowichan Bucktails, in recognition of this area as the origin of this special sport.

Vivid in my memory is the first coho I hooked on a bucktail fly while at the Salmon Point kelp bed. I can still see the high V wake of water boring down on my fly as the coho came in to strike. Hooked on the trailer fly, he cartwheeled and sky-walked behind the boat, outlined in the silver froth of the motor wake against the silhouette of dark blue water. The heavily pulsating rod in my hand as meters and meters of line screamed from the single action reel firmly convinced me this was one of the premier salmon fishing experiences on the west coast!

In recent years, as I have experimented with a wide variety of salmon fly patterns, I have found that bucktailing gives me that much-needed confidence in my flies. Unlike the traditional bucktail fly, with its keel and trailer hooks, I have found that single hooks are just as effective. I prefer a stainless steel hook, Mustad 34007 or 34011, as they will not tarnish after repeated use in salt water and long waits in my fly box. I prefer sizes number 2, 1 and 1/0, although I do tie flies up to number 5/0 for this purpose. I emphasize silver simplicity in my patterns. I have found that thin strands of material tied directly on the hook without tail, body or hackle are very effective. For variety, I recommend experimenting with strands of color, or tinsel bodies but, above all else, *keep it simple*—herring do not have hackles! Silver-bodied fry are the primary salmon feed and this is what you try to imitate to decoy these highly exciting sport fish.

My experimentation while bucktailing has given me a solid base of patterns I know will catch salmon. As the season advances and I am able to take up traditional anchoring and fly casting methods, I *know* these patterns will hook fish.

Casting

When open water casting, fishing from an anchored boat is the most successful technique. I like to compare the tidal currents of the sea with those often visible on the surface of a river. For those anglers who have used a shooting head or a wet line in a river, fishing for winter steelhead, the action of the fly line in salt water is very familiar, but with the one added and most crucial dimension of retrieving directly underneath. As with river wet line fishing, the object is to get the fly down to a certain depth. To establish the direction of the line drift after you have anchored, use the traditional river fifteen-meter upstream cast, followed by a mend. Yes, a line mend!

Casting Distance

As all fly fishermen know, distance is never a vital ingredient for hooking fish rather, it is the retrieve, the enticement of the morsel offered, that makes the fish strike. Saltwater salmon fly fishing requires longer leaders than those used for most fishing. This is a direct result of the clear water you will generally fish. These leaders often become cumbersome on the cast, so keep your tip up on the back and forecast!

Casting Locations

Bait fish locations and salmon feeding behavior dictate specific feeding locations. Anchor near schools of bait fish concentrated near kelp and cast into them. Feeding salmon either swim below or at the edge, of bait fish schools.

Clear Your Stripping Area

What fly fisherman has never felt the agony of losing a good fish because he stepped on his fly line in the bottom of the boat? With salmon, this is one of those inevitable occurrences that, after it has happened just once, will forever make the angler check on each retrieve to ensure the bottom is clear of any object that may snag his line when a salmon runs. Remember, I warned you!

Finger Protection on the Retrieve

Salt water is very abrasive when the fly line is drawn over fingers during the retrieves. I am certain some ingenious inventor will soon market an effective finger glove for anglers who spend time fly fishing in salt water. In the meantime carry a full pack of Band-Aids and place these on your fingers where the line is continually stripped. Be certain to put them on before you start so you are accustomed to the line being stripped over a less sensitive area when a fish strikes.

Fishing Locations

Make a habit of cruising those proven areas where sport boats concentrate. While there, search for bait school concentrations before you anchor. These areas are often at the edge of a reef on the tidal corner of an island. It is noteworthy that the southeast corner of the Gulf Islands are usually highly productive salmon locations. When you cruise on tidal flats of twenty meters or less, concentrate on kelp or isolated shallow rock formations

Flotsam Beware

Flotsam is a common hazard for anyone fly fishing on salt water. Tide line accumulation of floating items and constantly drifting beach debris drastically reduce an effective cast, yet it is a common element the saltwater fly fisherman meets on virtually every trip. Often, floating weed will tear off on a back cast, but listen to the sound of your fly as it comes past—anything out of the ordinary must be checked. Eel grass is particularly frustrating because it will not tear off like common sea lettuce. One trick that will often work is to leave your line and fly in the water on a false power back cast. In the water, the fly will tear through weed without breaking off the leader, permitting the angler to continue fishing without lengthy interruption.

Flotsam is a Magnet

If there is any object floating on the surface, it is uncanny how salmon and your fly line will eventually tangle with that object. Floating debris acts like a magnet when fighting fish around your boat. Be constantly aware of surface debris and try to guide your fish away.

Fly Fishing Flag

I am continually astounded at how being at anchor draws other fishermen, bait fishermen are particularly embarrassing. I have had experiences where they have bumped my anchored boat in their zeal to rake bait, hooked their rake into my fly line and tangled on my anchor rope. Yes, the waters are open to all, but there are common courtesies. I suggest that anchored fly fishermen fly a flag indicating they are fly fishing, as do scuba divers, just to let other anglers know what they are doing.

Herring = Salmon!

One does not need to be a mathematician to know the formula: herring = salmon! If you have ever been saltwater fishing, you know that the most important ingredient for success is to fish in areas where the bait fish are. Boats equipped with depth sounders/fish finders cruise continually, looking for schools of bait fish. If they are bait fishing or drift fishing, they know that being in the location of a bait school will offer the greatest chance of catching a salmon.

Hooks

Always use stainless steel hooks to tie your saltwater flies. In my earlier experimentation years, I used a variety of wet, nickel-plated and bronze hooks that, if I neglected to wash and dry carefully after every trip, always stained the light-colored materials (bucktail, fishair, polar bear hair) I used. Even if I simply left them, supposedly dry, in my fly box they seemed to stain the materials. I now tie all my patterns on a stainless steel hook, concentrating on Mustad and Tru

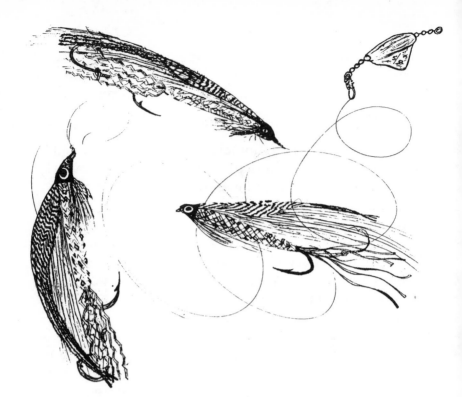

Turn sizes and know I can rest easy when my fly box is closed for any length of time.

Hunt to Find Feeding Salmon

At the start of each fishing trip, hunt for feeding salmon. Too often, sport anglers will go to known "fishing spots" and ignore Nature's signals telling where the feeding salmon are. One signal—the hovering dip-diving Bonaparte's gulls—are a sure sign that feeding salmon are chasing bait fish to the surface.

Throughout, I have referred to the need for the fly fisher to move when activity slows. This is the act of *salmon hunting.* Every time I head out on the water, I am constantly watching the surface signs to find the salmon concentrations. Salmon are migrating fish in a daily changing environment, due to bait fish, winds, tides, storms and light. To be consistently successful, the fly fisher must continually change location.

Let Them Run!

Salmon are powerful fish in open water. Even a small twenty-five-centimeter grilse will pull line from your reel. Regardless of your tippet strength, let them run! This certainly adds to the excitement, but it also ensures you will be able to fight the fish from the reel; an imperative for success with saltwater salmon. A minimum of 200 meters of backing is one of those absolute musts.

Location, Location, Location

If there is one truism for saltwater salmon fly fishing it would be the same as the number-one truism for real estate sales, "Location, location, location!" Salmon in salt water are opportunistic, migrating fish, not resident trout in a lake. The saltwater fly fisherman must make this quantum mental change if he is to be consistently successful.

Patience!

If you are in an area where other salmon anglers are catching fish by drift fishing or bait fishing, be patient—it is usually only a matter of time before a feeding salmon decides to take your fly.

Persistence

I have often spent hours anchored in one location without a single strike. My only reward during those times was the knowledge I gained of my natural surroundings, which I have always found invaluable. Bait movement and bird activity have added to that base of knowledge which I know has given me the confidence I now feel when fly fishing. During many of these blank days, salmon may have come in singles and, on occasion, I have had dramatic strikes, like the nine-kilogram chinook that took my fly while I was demonstrating saltwater techniques to a boatfull of fly fishermen.

Retrieve of Your Fly Line

Erratic, slow and short; this is the best description for the salmon retrieve. I use the strip retrieve, drawing the line along my right index finger while my right hand holds the rod. When I have a strike I cinch the line in my index finger while using my right wrist and hand to lift the rod tip and set the hook.

I will often experiment with a new retrieve, always trying to find that single, most effective, retrieve. Invariably I find I will continue with the standard short, slow and erratic strip retrieve. This seems to be the most effective, with the salmon strike being a simple take.

Rust!

Salt water is extremely corrosive on fly reels, flies, knives and other metal items so must be checked and cleaned on a regular basis. I have found this to be true even for so-called salt-proof reels. It is amazing how even the smallest parts oxidize!

Shooting Heads

When fishing in salt water, from three to fifteen meters, I have found shooting heads the most effective. This is particularly true anchored near a kelp bed where the midtide action is that of a fast-moving river. A number ten or eleven shooting head, attached to thirty meters of extra-fast running wet line is very effective for feeding salmon.

Skip Fly Bucktailing

In recent years skip fly bucktailing has become a modern adaptation of the traditional bucktailing method. Fishing guides effectively use this method to ensure the V wake strike of coho and the occasional chinook for their clients.

In this method the boat moves at a speed that keeps the trolled fly skimming just under the surface. Once the speed is established, with the rod tip pointing at the fly, the angler repeatedly pulls his rod tip toward the front of the boat, horizontal to the water, effectively skipping the fly out of the water. He then points his rod to the back of the boat which, in turn, lays the fly in the water in a crippled fashion. The traveling boat soon picks up the slack line and the process is repeated. Most strikes seem to come just as the angler is beginning to pull the fly. Strikes are usually visible and *dramatic!* Guides caution beginners to hold tight or the rod can pull right out of their hands when a fish takes the fly. It is another method of testing the effectiveness of your patterns for anchored casting.

Strikes!

I have always found that the salmon strike of a fly is unique in fly fishing. For coho and chinook, it is simply a sudden stop of the fly line—but what a stop! It seems I have hooked a large, solid, immovable object. Rarely is there the smash strike one associates with an active, feeding trout, although these do occur and they are dramatic but generally, the fly line simply stops on a retrieve. Occasionally, the salmon will then slowly come with the fly line, surfacing as it questions the object in its mouth. With this strike, the fly fisherman has only a moment to check his retrieved line to be certain it is clear of boat bottom snags before the salmon makes its first long dash for freedom.

Tide Knowledge

Tides have a dramatic affect on the activity of bait fish, hence on salmon feeding activity. Become knowledgeable about the tides in your various fly fishing spots and, in particular, how each affects bait fish movement. Salmon feed on various tides; coho, usually on a flood, while chinook usually feed just before, during and after slack tides. Rapid currents during midflood or midebb tides often force bait fish close to shore or close to an anchoring position for the fly fisherman. It has been my experience that, with new tides, it will often take two days for a particular salmon feeding pattern to be established.

Working the tides, the speed at which the water is moving, is one skill, like mending your fly line during river fishing, which must be mastered for greatest success. I have found it necessary, when two people are fishing from an anchored boat, to change places on a regular basis. This allows each angler the opportunity to work his fly most effectively while countering the tidal drift under the boat. Changing places, the front and back casting areas, should also be a standard practice when you have to contend with a strong wind.

Weighted Flies

In my fly box, I carry a selection of weighted flies of those patterns that have taken salmon. During a day of fishing, tides create water currents where even shooting heads will not keep your fly at the salmon depths. During these times, I will change to these weighted patterns.

Wind Knots

Wind knots in your leader are likely the most common reason for loosing a hooked fish. After many such experiences I now make it a habit to check my leader after a set number of casts, running my fingers along the full length of the leader to feel for any abrasions caused by flotsam or from the constant wind knots. Salmon are powerful fish and any abrasion, no matter how small, must mean a new leader!

Window Cast

Salmon rarely rise as trout will, but my experience

has taught me that the *window* remains if you cast quickly enough to the location where a salmon has jumped or surfaced. Crippled bait fish appear to often lose control of their air bladder, so they will scurry along just under the surface. To a salmon, they are a certain meal that will see a salmon rise to the surface. When this occurs, prepare your dry line outfit and cast to that window. A fly quickly cast to this surface action will often take a salmon the moment the fly hits the water!

8

Salmon and Angler Management

This chapter provides an opportunity for me to discuss several areas where my involvement and experiences have given me a specific view. In 1976, when the Canadian government announced the Salmonid Enhancement Program, I became active as a member of the Salmonid Enhancement Task Group, the public body given the task of overseeing this mas-

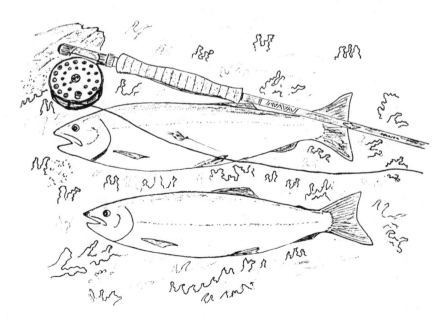

sive program aimed at bringing Salmonid species back to their historic 1900s numbers. Since that time, I have continued to sit on this task group, both as a delegate and an alternate.

Preserve the Opportunity to "Angle!"

I have one primary fear haunting me throughout each year: will my angling opportunity be regulated away? Will the managers do as they have done in the past and create blanket regulations, fin fish closures, that will take away my opportunity to fish? The site-specific fin fish closure regulation was initially proclaimed for conservation of one salmon species only—the chinook. Certainly, this form of management has made it easy to regulate all fishermen, but it is all-encompassing and has resulted in the loss of many fine salmon and other fin fish angling opportunities.

I strongly believe the salmon and saltwater sport angler is being irrationally regulated to the point where angling will no longer be a right and responsibility but a narrow privilege for a select few. I believe the right to angle should never be lost to any regulation. It is the sport fisher's and the fisheries manager's greatest responsibility to ensure this right will always exist. I have no difficulty with rational management regulations for tackle and those that provide various limited-entry needs but, the right to angle must never be regulated away!

Sadly, we have seen the beginning of irrational blanket management, with the spot area closures that restrict all fin fishing in designated areas of the coast. A chinook closure for *conservation* reasons—Yes! A *blanket* closure that restricts *all* saltwater angling—No!

152

Creeks are for Coho and Kids!

Fortunately, Canadian fisheries managers have recognized this basic affinity and have produced a, Salmonids in the Classroom program for the British Columbia school curriculum.

I have been fortunate to have been a part of this program, even to the point of Adopting-A-Stream. Over the years, I have watched community attitudes change so much that fish are now a recognized part of our wildlife heritage.

In my profession as an educator I have assisted in the creation of several small stream curriculum-related programs that were adopted as educational tools. These have been a highlight of my educational career, for I know the stewardship of the resource will be in the hands of a much more sensitive generation. They know the salmon is a species at the pinnacle of freshwater predator-prey relationships. We could say salmon are a keystone species in the north Pacific Rim. Investments in education are blue chip stocks ensuring the future's adults can make those hard, but necessary, species enhancement, preservation, conservation and management decisions. The next generation recognizes these fish as a barometer of a healthy stream and, through the many educational programs now available, they will ensure the future of these magnificent salmonids.

Small Stream Environmental Protection

Small streams with anadromous salmonids, whether tributaries of larger systems or complete watersheds, must receive the highest priority for environmental protection.

In recent years there has been a wellspring of recognition that, in fact, the river is but the highway for migrating salmonids. The vital nurseries for salmonids are the small streams, the tributaries and the upper headwaters. Coupled with this recognition is also the knowledge that, at one time, every small stream in the Pacific Northwest with unhindered access to the sea held a native population of salmonid species.

Unfortunately, because of the size of these small systems, industry has been brutal with these small salmonid nurseries. Also, urban development has been equally brutal, with impassable culverts, roads, channelization and other developments that have destroyed the unique races of salmonids in these nursery creeks.

Fortunately, in many cases, these small systems are still capable of providing rearing habitat and, in some cases, very specific fisheries. Governments at all levels must apply and insist upon protective measures for these small systems and incorporate covenants, ensuring no future destruction by industry or urban development.

Stream Bank Conservation Belt

The umbilical lifeline of every salmon watershed, its protective greenbelt, is still open to virtually every abuse of exploitation and development. Volumes have been written on the critical importance of stream bank vegetation to protect the integrity of streams. The conclusion in every report states emphatically that a strip of mature vegetation must be preserved to protect the well-being of the stream, to protect the stream's aesthetic and recreational value and to protect its fish and wildlife populations.

Specifically, a stream bank greenbelt protects deciduous species, particularly the alder, the major contributor of nitrogen in the ecosystem of the watershed. It provides shade and shelter, minimizing water temperature increases and acts as a filter to prevent sediment from entering the water system. It provides a buffer from overland run-off water and acts as a catch basin against debris from this run-off. It prevents direct solar radiation and protects the area from direct precipitation impact. It maintains adequate oxygen levels for all stream life and provides the major food stuff or biomass for fish. It provides protective access for fish to their spawning grounds. It provides a profusion of plant growth rich in nutrients for wildlife and a corridor for migrating wildlife from their summer pastures to their wintering grounds. In short, stream bank vegetation is the lifeline of the watershed.

When will we see protective legislation to protect this lifeline?

Fish must have Legal Rights to Water in British Columbia

Incredible as it sounds, in British Columbia, fish do not have a legal right to the use of water. It is imperative that legislation be enacted that *guarantees* fish their basic need—water. This legislation must include protection in the form of water quality standards and minimum flow requirements.

Commercial Fishery

Volumes could be written and have been written about the historical and traditional commercial salmon fishery. It is a vital industry, with many traditions that cannot simply be dismissed without considerable planning. I believe that, in many areas of the Pacific Northwest, terminal estuary commercial fisheries must be the management technique of the future. The salmon resource is too finite to continue with the historic forms we have witnessed in the past. In areas like the Strait of Georgia, no commercial net or troll fishery should occur except at estuary areas, when commercial fishermen are targeting on-site specific stocks of salmon.

The definition of commercial salmon fishing should be *the use of the salmon resource for profit.* In this definition I would include all users who receive payment in their exploitation of the resource. This would include salmon sport fishing resorts, salmon fishing guides, sporting goods and other stores selling salmon sport and commercial fishing tackle, magazines publishing salmon sport or commercial advertising, salmon fishing writers and authors, hotels and motels catering to sport anglers and commercial fishermen—all support industries receiving a direct revenue from this resource. Doing this is but an administrative task likely easier than we might fear. A fin fish fee has been considered in the past that might apply directly to those areas where a salmon is evident. In others, a surtax could be applied, based on a percentage of involvement. Complicated? Yes, likely so, but the resource is delicate and must be managed, not regulated. In the creel, those who profit must pay!

Beach Ethics

When pressure from other anglers builds in a particular area, what are the alternatives? So far, this particular problem does not exist in most shallow beach areas but it is growing and will soon have to be faced in terms of angler ethics.

One memorable day, while I was fishing inside a kelp bed off Francisco Point, I continued to be pressured by three guide boats bucktailing or slow-trolling small herring. I had action on my fly during the morning that was obvious to the sport fleet working their various salmon fishing methods outside the kelp; suffice it to say they were also into several good coho.

The problem I had however, was with the three guide boats who, on seeing me anchored, alone and rather obvious inside the kelp, continued to motor in long concentric circles around me, coming to within a double-cast-length of my position. Their circular routes would bring one of the boats inside the kelp near my anchored boat every ten minutes or less. Their effect on my fishing was obvious—the moment a boat came toward the edge of the small herring the coho were feeding on, the herring would dash toward me for the safety of the kelp beyond casting reach, making the coho simply disappear. Gone were the delayed surface roils of panic stricken herring as were the occasional leaping jack coho that seemed to feed continually in these shallows.

It would take many minutes for the herring school to return and settle in the previous area but this was often not the case and they were simply gone, schooled in another area. This forced me to lift the anchor and paddle to a new location, if it was available but, once the herring school appeared and the salmon roils began again, it was just minutes before the next guide boat motored in, scaring the fish away again.

Fortunately, this experience has only occurred on the odd occasion, although it is becoming more frequent. Ethics are not to be regulated but what should anglers do in these circumstances? For the fly fisherman, an intruding boat effectively halts all success.

What are our Future Genetic Options?

I am deeply concerned about the possibility we could be creating single stock salmonids, with the continued emphasis on hatchery production for coho and chinook. We know the egg-to-smolt survival from hatchery production, at 80 to 90 percent, far exceeds

that of nature's 5 to 10 percent. Have we protected and preserved our options? Variability is the life-blood, the very future of salmonids. Where is this variability now that we are into fifth-generation coho and third-generation chinook hatchery stock? Have we established a gene bank to preserve those unique river, stream and creek salmonids? What are our genetic options to ensure future species' viability and variability?

Volunteers!

Have you done your part? Are you a member of an organized group who will effect change for our salmon resources?

While speaking in Japan at a Salmonid Educational Symposium, I was overwhelmed by questions about British Columbia's salmonid volunteers. I had related that British Columbia has over 8,000 volunteers working on community salmonid enhancement projects, varying from classroom incubators to impressive hatcheries. This concept was new in their personal attitudes toward the fishery resource but it is one that dominates our affinity for the salmonid resource.

Freshwater Fishing for all Salmon Species

In other areas of the book, I have highlighted the fact that some species are forbidden for the freshwater angler, specifically chums, sockeye and pinks in river systems. Reading the federal and provincial regulations, you will note that there are other closures as well for coho and chinook. In all my discussions with federal managers, I have yet to have a rational reason for these closures except on those rare occasions when a specific stock requires a closure for conservation reasons.

This blanket closure of salmon species to the freshwater angler has, sadly, been adopted by present federal fisheries managers into the standard blanket fin fish closures now choking the angler and the regulations booklet.

The provincial government must submit its fishing regulations to Ottawa for approval, usually two years in advance. It is of concern to note the provincial fisheries managers have, in the past, requested adult salmon angling for species other than coho and chinook in British Columbia rivers but have been turned down by the federal approval board. We must ask why. What rational reasons are possible for this gross waste of a valuable recreational resource? If we truly have fisheries management, where is the site-specific, stock-specific management program for the recreational angler?

With the advent and success of the Salmonid Enhancement Program, the time has come to change these antiquated regulations and allow anglers the op-

159

portunity to experience all freshwater adult salmon as a game species.

Public involvement is forever being used as a management need for the salmonid resource. The freshwater angler, given his rightful opportunity to fish for all salmon species, will provide an army of river guardians who will ensure preservation of the stream environment and the stocks.

The resource is here; the anglers are here; where is fisheries management?

Turning the Tide

In closing this chapter, I would like to quote my dedication for a lengthy and detailed salmon sport fishing and environmental presentation I prepared for the Commission on Pacific Fisheries Policy, headed by Dr. Peter Pearce. I feel it is as appropriate today as it was a decade ago:

To the anglers of the twenty-first century:
May you recognize that we have tried,
That the streams still harbor salmonids,
That the resource remains public,
That social-historic traditions have been preserved,
That angling opportunity has never been lost,
That your future still provides the challenge of an unknown river,
That we have preserved the options,
That water, in its natural environment, remains inviolate,
And, that the presence of fish is still the measure of a healthy environment!

9

Eternal Memories

Quadra Island Coho Fly Fishing

The wealth of memories we all hold about those trips that were particularly successful or resulted in a special bond or initiated a quantum thought are the spice of any outdoor sport. Saltwater salmon fly fishing has rewarded me with many of these special memories, the more indelible because I have felt an almost pioneering satisfaction with this unique form of fly fishing with which I have been experimenting.

Etched firmly in my mind is one specific trip and it is for this reason I wish to share it with the readers. It is an experience with father and sons; with silver, struggling salmon; with weather, wind and water; and it represents many of the situations probable and possible while saltwater salmon fly fishing.

British Columbia's northern Strait of Georgia seasonally hosts an infinite multitude of silver salmon, numbering like crystal snowflakes in a winter storm. From the open Pacific Ocean, salmon of all five species race south through the turbulent, cold waters of Johnstone Strait on the inside of Vancouver Island, through the pinched channel of Seymour Narrows, finally out Discovery Passage, to the northern wide, calm waters of the Strait of Georgia.

This is an ancient route used by Salmonids between glacial ages, with the most recent species evolved since the last glacial period, ten thousand years ago. With its immense silver bounty, it is a route which modern man has only now come to comprehend. At times the flow of fish appears endless, as they respond to nature's migration triggers for the final stage of their aquatic odyssey. These salmon runs peak during midsummer and, like an hourglass, steadily fill the Strait of Georgia.

At the entrance to the Strait of Georgia, a vast smorgasbord of marine feed prevails that, fortunately for the angler, detains many of the sport salmon—the coho, pink and chinook, for short feeding periods. It is here, off the southern tip of Quadra Island, that these salmon adjust to new currents and sort the many river smells of the strait before realigning their homing instinct to that single ultimate goal, spawning in their natal stream.

Prevailing heavy coastal storms hammer the full

coast of the Pacific Northwest most months of the year, buffered by the land mass of Vancouver Island. On the British Columbia mainland, towering coastal mountains check these storms in the winter but in the summer, when the traditional large high pressure area prevails over the Pacific Northwest, they also create local northwest winds, funneling down the many river valleys, the fjords of the Coast Mountain Range, to join over the many islands at the north end of the strait and gently caress the waters of this most *fishy* area.

These summer northwest winds played a significant role in a saltwater salmon fly fishing experience forever etched in my mind. This experience expelled forever the nagging myth that coho salmon in salt water will not consistently strike a cast fly. They did and, for six unforgettable mornings, my arm ached as I lived a fly fisher's adrenaline high!

Several other significant natural phenomena occur during the summer in this area and combine to create the ideal conditions for this unique, exciting fly fishing experience.

Quadra Island lies at the northern end of the strait. This is a large gulf island with shallows at its southern end growing a profusion of marine life providing feed for the salmon and other smaller sea life in the salmon's food chain.

During midsummer, small, juvenile herring abound in this area, growing on this continually available smorgasbord. The numerous kelp beds throughout the area provide necessary shelter for these prime salmon bait fish.

At specific times during midsummer, but only for short periods, an algae bloom occurs, darkening the surface water throughout the area. The water turns a deep brownish-green, severely limiting visibility and provides additional escape cover, spreading the herring throughout the area. Southerly migrating coho, pink and chinook salmon schools pause here, concentrating off the southern beaches of Quadra Island, as they orient themselves for their further migrations south through the Strait of Georgia.

Low tides add one further set of environmental conditions at this time of year, as they drop more each morning until the full moon change, when they will begin to increase in daily heights.

These tides, in combination with the other factors—salmon migration, northwest winds, algae bloom and bait fish—all provide the necessary combination of factors, the special ingredients for this incredible fly fishing. Add a determined angler and we have a fly fisherman's utopia.

The beach area on the southern end of Quadra Island is typical cobblestone. At the south end of this cobblestone beach, where sand and rocks meet in the intertidal zone, occasional small-boat size boulders litter the area. These large, protruding boulders played an important role for this fly fisherman, for it was around these the herring concentrated and seemingly excited the feeding coho.

The combination of environmental factors that provided the opportunity for successfully working a number eight, six-meter sink-tip fly line, seemed to occur just after the high tide began to ebb. As the tide receded, it exposed a large point of land with these numerous boulders, ending at Francisco Point. Heavy northwest winds blow down Sutil Channel on the east side of Quadra Island, appearing to clear the algae bloom from the shallow water near the beach for short distances of up to fifty meters. The water in this area was sparkling clear, but fading as it reached the murky brown-green of the algae bloom farther out.

Schools of young herring concentrated in this very shallow area, possibly pushed there by the schools of cruising, voraciously feeding coho in the deeper waters.

It was here, in this same area two summers previous, that I had first come upon these factors. Fishing with my two young sons, we had found coho in small schools and in singles, cruising through the concentrated herring and periodically slashing out to feed. At that time, we were fishing with light trout casting rods and six-pound test line. I would motor my four-meter boat to within a few meters of the large boulders in water no more than a meter deep. We cast toward shore or parallel to the beach, using high speed retrieve spinning reels and eight or twelve gram Stingzelda lures (herring imitations) or small white Buzz Bombs. A fast retrieve was a must, otherwise the lure would snag on the cobblestone shallows. More often than not, we would snag herring, as we rapidly retrieved our lures through these waters. During that first summer, our success on coho was high but, understandably, expensive in lures. On occasion, I would take the fly rod to the area but the circumstances were never just right, or so I thought. If they would take the cast lure in these shallows, surely a cast fly would work as well.

Success with winter steelhead fly fishing, pink salmon fly fishing and October stream and beach coho fly fishing in other areas and continual conversations with other anglers had provided me with several fly patterns with which I had some confidence for these silver coho. During previous years I had tried fly fishing in the area but I now know that conditions were

165

not correct, limiting my success to a few jacks, grilse and the rare coho but, this particular summer, I was *prepared*. When word came that the coho had arrived on that July 16th, two days earlier than the previous year, I launched my four-meter Ripmaster boat—a Whaler model—and crossed Discovery Passage, heading for the Frisco shallows. I again equipped myself with light spinning gear, should the fly fishing not succeed, but this time I also took a number eight, six-meter sink-tip fly line, my three-meter Hardy fly rod, and a Hardy Marquis saltwater fly reel, supported by 200 meters of braided nylon backing.

On that first day, I arrived to find about fifty sport boats already trolling the area, but in deep water, well away from the shallows. A building northwest wind was blowing down Sutil Channel but only a few knots in strength at that time of the early morning. As I neared the shallows, I throttled back to a dead slow, watching for the scattered boulders just under the surface, camouflaged by the dark algae-clogged water. I finally stopped near a large flat-topped rock and dropped the anchor in the midst of a bottom-blackening school of young herring. No other anglers were close by, although the point held three commercial sport boats with single anglers fishing with bobbers and live herring. As I watched, two of these commercial anglers were suddenly into salmon.

Unlimbering my fly tackle, I threaded the line through the rod eyes, then opened the fly box to select what would become the moment of truth. The fly I chose was one I'd had some success with beach fishing for coho off the estuary of Black Creek in October. It was completely pink and tied like a sedge pattern with a beetle back but no hackle. At the eye of the hook, two silver bead swivels created eyes, forming a pink optic fly.

This choice of fly was instrumental, during the coming week, in breaking the color barrier needed to lure the coho to strike. During previous trips, I had used traditional herring imitations of a silver body and green, but with only limited success. Earlier in the spring, while fly fishing for bluebacks, I had found a decided attraction to pink in these immature coho and reasoned that this color preference would continue with adult fish. Numerous shrimp abound in the Strait of Georgia and these constitute a very major diet for young coho and, often, for adults. It was reasonable, then, to assume that the ghost shrimp living in the shallow, inter-tidal sands would be a target for coho and the Pink Optic Fly imitated these.

I tied on a long, six-pound test leader of about four meters in length and began to cast to the shallows, where a few coho were chasing the uncountable herring. The long leader was very necessary in salt water; my experiences with coho beach fly fishing had taught me it was needed to not spook the coho.

I was casting into the wind and soon realized the futility of that as line, leader or fly repeatedly tangled. I shifted position in the four-meter, flat-bottomed boat, which I had, years earlier, affectionately dubbed the *fishing machine* and began to cast with the wind. A continual splattering sound of dimpling herring was periodically punctuated by the sudden plop of leaping herring scattering from cruising coho or the sudden rush of roiling water as a coho slashed along the surface. My casting and retrieving of the fly line became methodical and I soon reached a rhythmic pattern, broken only when I tried to cover a surfacing coho or a shower of bait fish.

The first strike bent the rod tip almost to the water as a prime three-kilogram coho smashed the fly, snatching line and, almost, the rod out of my hand. I had a split second to check the loose line stripped in at my feet, then it was gone through my fingers and he was at the reel. In a rising crescendo, the reel scream snapped heads to attention in passing sport boats, then the fish paused. I felt the head-shaking shudder as he tested the resistance of line, leader and hook then, again, the ecstatic crescendo. By now, he was near the trolling sport boats a hundred meters away, but he held. The slow, dogged retrieve began then, as I caught my second wind. Eventually, back near the boat, he arched his spine, like a river trout using the current and slowly circled the boat. Then, close, he dogged near the cobblestone bottom, scattering the schools of herring as he finally came to the net.

When finally boated he was beautiful; a deep coho, silver bright and shimmering. This was the first! Truly, only the dedicated angler knows the thrill of finally putting together the many natural factors and equipment leading to success.

Ten minutes later, a second coho took the fly but, without the long run. He began a sustained fight, taking many minutes before he tired. With this second fish, I knew I had the right combinations and that euphoria of confidence set in. The third fish took a long time coming, at least an hour after the second, but three missed strikes between convinced me all was well.

By now, the fly was badly askew, with bead eyes sliding continually around the head of the fly. I opted for a second pattern then—the Pink Minnow. This second fly combined the important pink color with a silver body. Soon, it also brought a strike and it was here that the Pink Minnow became my second certain fly.

The second morning, I arrived at the shallows beneath the Quadra Island bluffs at 7:30 A.M., just before the tide began to ebb. I watched two mature bald eagles settle on rocks near Butler's Point, then I began to cruise in the bay, searching for showering herring. Again, well over fifty sport and sport-guide boats were trolling in the deeper water, off the edge of the many kelp beds in the area.

In minutes, I spotted numerous showering herring in one particular small bay. The coho were obviously in a school and moving slowly through the bay, judging from the number of showering roils of herring.

I moved slowly toward the bay, stopping just at

casting range from the infinite herring. I dropped anchor and drifted slowly with the tide, parallel to shore, until the anchor line tightened. I started to cover the boiling herring with lengthening casts and was soon dropping the Pink Minnow fly near a large boulder just beginning to be exposed from the ebbing tide. As I slowly strip retrieved the fly past the rock, it stopped! I lifted the rod tip and the sight of a large coho with open mouth and shaking head, lifting to the surface was astonishing. The fish came toward the boat with the fly clearly embedded in the side of its mouth. I frantically stripped in fly line as fast as possible to gather in the slack as the fish came toward me but it was not possible and he was free, leaving the fly sitting in the water only to skim across the surface as I finally reached the end of the slack line.

Checking the fly, I proceeded to once again send out casts farther and farther, reaching to the far side of the rock, where young herring continued to shower. Within moments, the fly stopped as before. Again, a hooked coho came to the surface, moving toward the boat, slowly shaking his head but this time I had the slack and the sudden resistance turned the fish. He started a long run out, toward the kelp beds in the deeper water. When, at last, I brought him close to the boat, a piece of floating kelp snagged the line, the long stem on the end of the kelp bulb acting as a lever for the fish, resulting in a few minutes of intense care with line and leader, until the kelp drifted past with the tide. The fish came in then but, ever so slowly, circled several times, with numerous short runs under the boat. With one last leap, a common habit of coho, he finally rolled over on his side, ready at last, for the net.

What happened then was a repeat of the day before, with limited but continual strikes. By midtide the bite began to die off as I placed my fourth fish in the boat, taken this time on a red carnation streamer fly.

Day three dawned clear as before and, after a light breakfast with my son Barry, we headed up-island from Comox to launch at Big Rock. It was a forty-minute drive from the house to the launch, an ideal time to plan strategy. The weather forecast was similar to the previous day and, providing herring, tides, wind, algae bloom and coho were similar, the day's success was also predictable.

Crossing Discovery Passage, we noticed several sport boats working the back eddy of the Cape Mudge lighthouse. This was a certain sign there was a fresh run of salmon. When we reached the waters off the Quadra bluffs, the armada of sport boats presented itself once again, trolling in the outer kelp waters, with a few anchored nearer the shore, bobber fishing with live or strip herring.

Once again, I anchored near surfacing herring, off one of the major boulders in the area. My son is an experienced, skilled and dedicated fly fisherman and we were soon casting well out to the area where the coho were working.

While the day was predictable, the action was not! During the first hour, six fish took solidly but were on-off fish until 7:30 A.M. when the first fish was hooked to stay. The power of this coho was incredible as he took the fly on a smashing run, then headed straight out to the open water. In the lengthy, dogged fight that followed, he unerringly stayed in the reflected sunlight and almost got away when he wrapped the line around a flotsam of seaweed. Weighing in the two-kilogram range, he was a twin to those we had caught on previous days.

Barry's first coho came a few minutes later and was one of the few real tail-walking jumpers we caught. A few minutes into the fight, a guide boat swung in close to shore and began circling toward the leaping coho. Our frantic signals and yells drew little response but, fortunately, his close circling missed crossing Barry's line.

It is a credit to the guide boats in the area—and there were many—that only on that one occasion during the six days, did they intrude on our angling. Small sport commercial boats, on the other hand, were a continual intrusion, often cruising in the bays close to shore and spooking the feeding schools of salmon.

When Barry's fish finally came near the boat, it was difficult to tell who was the most exhausted—Barry or the coho. The tension of a continually leaping fish, the guide boat's intrusion and, at the last, a snagged piece of seaweed had Barry's nerves at a snapping edge but eventually the sawing edge of the nylon leader sliced through the seaweed and he finally boated the fish. Like the others, it was a prime silver beauty and, along with my first, filled the bottom of the plastic fish basin. Barry soon boated his second, then third, as the action picked up near our boat.

The salmon continued to boil close to the boat for some time, often, right beside it as they concentrated the schools of herring. These were the frustrating fish as they seemed to rarely take the fly. Rather, it was the apparent lone singles loafing near the flurry of action or slowly cruising under the herring that were the takers.

We could follow the movement of the coho schools by the showering herring. They would move parallel to the beach under the herring who, in turn, would blossom outward above them as they cruised by. Then, on some signal, the coho would slash at the herring, causing them to leap above the water by the boat or beside the boulders, where they had concentrated to escape. On numerous occasions near the boulders, we would see the slashing coho slide up and even, *over* the rocks in their frenzy to strike the panic-stricken, escaping herring. On two separate occasions I even saw coho herd the herring right to the shore and often, both coho and herring would thrash up on the beach in their excitement, flopping on the cobblestones before reaching the water again.

The excitement generated by these schools of salmon as they fed past the boat was highly infectious but frustrating, as they often ignored the flies cast in their midst. We later speculated that these must have been the fish that gave us the smashing strikes that seemed to tear the rod and line from our fingers. However, as I mentioned earlier, the majority of strikes were simply takes. The line would suddenly halt on the retrieve, snapping the rod tip down to the water's edge. Unlike the smaller fish, there was no give on the strikes, as these salmon were too heavy. They simply stopped the line, dead in the water.

As we began to lift the rod tip, following the strike, the fish would often appear just under the surface, shaking its head from side to side, trying to clear the hook. Once near the surface though, they would turn, begin a slow circle of the boat as they tested the resistance of the line, then, in a panic, dash for the deep water.

Constantly casting to these feeding, active schools, we began to experiment with different retrieves in the hope of finding the one that worked consistently. During most of our fishing we had used short continual ten- to fifteen-centimeter strips, dropping the fly line at our feet in a cleared space on the floor of the boat. We stripped the fly line through our right index fingers, closing them the moment we had a strike and we also found it effective to pause in midretrieve. Following a few short strips after the cast, we would pause and a fish would take when we began the short retrieve.

By noon of that third day the bite was off and we headed for home to recharge for the next day.

Days four and five were much the same as the first three days with few variations but two that did occur dealt with fish.

While fishing near one of the rocks, a coho struck with a frenzy that snapped three or more meters of retrieved fly line from the bottom of the boat. Then he was on the reel and going strong! When he finally halted, I could feel the line-twisting gyrations he was performing before I could begin to retrieve the line. This particular fish took a long time to come in and it wasn't until he was near the boat that we saw the reason why. In his gyrations following the initial run, he must have thrown the hook, but the line, which was twisted around his body, had snagged the hook at the tip of his tail as it unwound. This is a common occurrence when fighting large, active fish. On the retrieve, I was pulling this salmon to the boat tail first, a difficult feat with a struggling four-kilogram coho and six-pound test leader.

The other fish was typical of other strikes and runs. However, when we boated this particular fish we noted a clipped adipose fin, the small fin on the back between the dorsal fin and the tail that identifies fish of the salmonid family. This was obviously a hatchery coho, likely reared under the auspices of the Federal-Provincial Salmonid Enhancement Program or United States hatchery programs. The Canadian program began in 1976 aimed at doubling salmonid stocks throughout British Columbia to their levels at the turn of the century.

Near noon on day five the bite suddenly stopped and the herring seemed to have moved out to the kelp beds at Francisco Point. It was such an obvious change we moved to the shallow kelp bed hidden by the algae bloom and cast into its murky depths. At that time I was trying a small pink bucktail fly with two hooks, used more commonly for fast trolling with small spinners. I had cut off the keel hook with pliers, leaving only the trailer hook hidden upright in the sparse polar bear hair. We could occasionally see schools of herring in the kelp near the surface with the rare coho beneath. We hooked two good coho in the kelp, boated one and lost the other when he tangled the line in the kelp.

Day six held a change in the weather, with a light southeasterly wind rippling the water when we arrived. The algae bloom still darkened the water but the bait herring had left the shallows. A few small schools still persisted near the rocks, but no coho were evidenced by showering herring. The kelp bed held little promise, so we anchored near one of the rocks and began a methodical casting to those few herring. Sport boats in the area would come and go, constantly searching for the school of coho that had obviously moved, heading into the strait, pulled by the irresistible hereditary urge to return to their home river.

Almost at noon, one laggard coho turned into the herring school I was working and took my fly. With that one fish I relived all the previous days had given and vowed that, when once again these factors combined, I would be here reliving it all, over and over again.

Now, as I listen to the cassette tape of those six eventful days, it is with deep pleasure. The three-hour-long tape highlights the moments when fish were on or the times I paused in my casting to capture various experiences; the sounds of water and wind; the mewing of gulls and the screaming of eagles; the roar of outboards and guide-client talk; the plop of herring and the slash of coho; the visual and philosophic moments.

This experience convinced me that salmon in salt water will be consistently lured by a cast fly, ensuring the confidence I will need for further experimentation. This experimentation will take the route of tying new fly patterns, trying different types of fly lines, combining various environmental factors and natural phenomenon and, finally, searching out new locations where all of the above will again combine to feel that sudden halt of the fly line as a salmon strikes, then the seemingly endless run, that sudden euphoria—the nectar of the fly fisherman!